PORTER STANSBERRY

AMERICA
2020

THE SURVIVAL BLUEPRINT

FOREWORD BY
DR. RON PAUL

Published by Stansberry Research

Edited by Steven Longenecker and Fawn Gwynallen

About Stansberry Research

Founded in 1999 and based out of Baltimore, Maryland, Stansberry Research is the largest independent source of financial insight in the world. It delivers unbiased investment advice to self-directed investors seeking an edge in a wide variety of sectors and market conditions.

Stansberry Research has nearly two dozen analysts and researchers – including former hedge-fund managers and buy-side financial experts. They produce a steady stream of timely research on value investing, income generation, resources, biotech, financials, short-selling, macroeconomic analysis, options trading, and more.

The company's unrelenting and uncompromised insight has made it one of the most respected and sought-after research organizations in the financial sector. It has nearly one million readers and more than 400,000 paid subscribers in over 100 countries.

About the Author

Porter Stansberry founded Stansberry Research in 1999 with the firm's flagship newsletter, *Stansberry's Investment Advisory*.

Prior to launching Stansberry Research, Porter was the first American editor of the *Fleet Street Letter*, the world's oldest English-language financial newsletter.

Today, Porter is well-known for doing some of the most important – and often controversial – work in the financial-advisory business. Since he launched *Stansberry's Investment Advisory*, his string of accurate forecasts has made his advisory one of the most widely read in the world... and has helped his readers both avoid catastrophe and make incredible gains.

Table of Contents

Part IV
Secrets of the Silver Market

Part V
Goldscam: How to Protect Yourself and Grow Rich

Part VI
The World's Most Valuable Asset in a Time of Crisis

Part VII
**The Nine Most Important Things I'm Doing to Prepare
for a Crisis in America**

Part VIII
How to Own the World's Trophy Assets

Part IX
Porter Stansberry's Crash Course on How to Become a Better Investor

Part X
How You Can Earn Inflation-Proof, Crisis-Proof Income Streams in the Stock Market

One Final Thought:

———————————●———————————

Foreword

By Dr. Ron Paul

We're at a turning point in America.

Despite the stock market hitting record highs in 2015 and despite declining unemployment numbers, the dangers lurking in the economy today are greater than at any point since I started in Congress back in 1976.

We're no longer participating in a free market economy. And we're no longer using sound money. Asset prices move up and down at the whim of the Federal Reserve.

It's a sad fact that Washington now runs our economy and our monetary system.

By making trillions of dollars of credit available, it is conducting the largest monetary experiment in American history. Despite what the politicians say, they have no idea how it will all turn out.

You can ignore that ugly fact. But I hope you do not.

I hope you seek to neutralize the threats our dangerous monetary system has created. What you do will determine the fate of your family's financial future.

For your sake and the sake of our nation, I hope you choose to take action. I hope you save this copy of Porter Stansberry's book, *America 2020: The Survival Blueprint.*

This book is a must-read. I don't know of anyone who has spent as much time and money as Porter Stansberry figuring out how to protect yourself and prosper in the years to come.

You can't build economic growth or prosperity with a currency people don't have confidence in. But that's exactly what central banks are trying to do today.

The Fed and other central banks are trying to create prosperity out of thin air by printing money and debasing their currencies. It's an impossible task. More than that, *their actions will eventually cause a market crash worse than we saw in 2008.*

America 2020 will help you protect yourself from the catastrophe Porter and I both see coming. This book tells the story of how we got here... And why people are losing faith in our currency.

Most importantly, it tells you exactly how to prepare for the dangerous times ahead.

In this book, you'll find the knowledge you need to understand what's going on... and the ideas, techniques, and strategies you need to protect yourself and your family.

Porter and his team at Stansberry Research have already helped hundreds of thousands of investors see the truth about what is happening in America today. We hope you take this message seriously.

Best regards,

Dr. Ron Paul

Introduction
By Porter Stansberry

Stop... Before you read this book, I need to warn you.

I'm about to make some arresting claims about the future of our country.

I know this is a politically charged and emotional issue. My conclusions will not be easy for most readers to accept. Likewise, many of the things I am writing about will challenge people to re-examine what they believe about their country.

Understand, I am only writing about the facts as I find them. And the facts about America tell a painful story about a country in a steep decline, beset by problems of its own making.

I fear this publication will spark a tremendous amount of controversy. Many people will surely accuse me of deliberately writing inflammatory things to stir the pot and gain attention. That's not my intention. I've gone to great lengths throughout my career to protect my privacy.

I am speaking out because someone must. And I have the resources to do it. I am sharing these ideas with all who will listen because I know we have arrived at the moment of a long-brewing crisis.

I am only drawing conclusions based on the situation as it stands. I am not saying these conditions can't improve. Or that they won't improve.

The truth is, I am optimistic. While I believe our country is heading into a crisis, I also believe that... sooner or later... Americans will make the right choices and put our country back on sound footing.

Pay careful attention to the data I cite. And please send me corrections to the facts. I will happily publish any correction that can be substantiated. But please don't send me threats, accusations against my character, or baseless claims about my lack of patriotism. If I didn't love our country, none of these facts would upset me. I wouldn't have bothered writing this book.

It might not be pleasant to think about... but the figures I am going to present paint a sad, but accurate, picture: America is not the country it was 40 years ago. Our economy, politics, and culture have become dramatically warped.

I can't possibly analyze all the factors that have led to this decline, but I can document the core reasons we're in this situation and the prevailing symptoms that ail our country, our economy, and our people.

We've reached the point where we must fix what lies at the heart of America's decline. Our political leaders, our business leaders, and our cultural leaders have made a series of catastrophic choices... We cannot rely on them to fix what has been broken.

The damage can only be repaired by ordinary people who understand the problem and are willing to demand a solution.

With this knowledge in hand, I hope we can help to educate our families, neighbors, and leaders... We must encourage them to throw off the blinders of apathy and look at what is really happening to our country. We need to make choices that will put us back on the right path.

You see, the decline of our country is primarily a decline of our culture.

We have lost our sense of honor, humility, and the dedication to personal responsibility that, for more than 200 years, made our country the greatest hope for mankind. We have become a country of people who believe their well-being is someone else's responsibility.

These problems manifest in different ways across institutions in all parts of our society. But at their root, they are facets of the same stone. They are all part of the same essential problem.

The corruption of America isn't happening in one part of our country... or in one type of institution. It is happening across the landscape of our society, in almost every institution.

It's a kind of moral decay... a kind of greed... a kind of desperate grasp for power... And it's destroying our nation.

iv

I call it the "ethos of getting yours."

Americans know, in their bones, that something terrible is happening. Maybe you can't articulate it. Maybe you don't have the statistics to understand exactly what's going on. But my bet is, you think about it a lot.

It seems like everyone in our country has lost his moral bearing, from the highest government officials and senior corporate leaders all the way down to schoolteachers and local community leaders. The ethos of my fellow Americans seems to have changed from one of personal integrity and responsibility to "getting yours" – the all-out attempt, by any means possible, to get the most amount of benefits with the least amount of work.

You can see this in everything from the lowering of school standards to the widespread use of performance-enhancing drugs in professional, college, and high school sports. Cheating has become a way of life in America.

I have an idea about how this happened... about the root cause of this kind of corruption and why it was inevitable, given some of the basic facts regarding how we've organized our government and our corporations.

Problems that have warped our country are intertwined, but can be broken into three prevailing "corruptions"...

PART ONE

The Three Greatest Corruptions That Are Destroying America

Chapter 1

The Corruption of Politics

I'll start with one of the biggest factors in the decline of our civilization – the politics of entitlement.

It is routinely alleged in national political debates that something is fundamentally unfair and un-American about the huge "wealth gap" between the poorest and the wealthiest Americans.

Some politicians like to argue that the poor never have a real shot at the American dream. So as a nation, we owe them more and more of our resources to correct this injustice. Most important, *they claim only the government has the resources to correct this inequality.*

These are dangerous notions...

They promote a sense of entitlement. The American idea of entitlement argues that because you were born into a rich society, other people owe you something. The idea has become pervasive in our culture. It underlies the basic assumptions behind the idea of a "wealth gap."

Implicit is the assumption that successful Americans haven't rightfully earned their wealth... that in one way or another, they've taken advantage of the society and have an obligation to "give back" what they've "taken."

As you'll see, the idea of entitlement lies at the root of many of our most serious cultural problems.

The more obvious problem is the idea that the government is responsible for fixing the "wealth gap." But the government has proven wholly ineffective at dealing with poverty in America. The data is conclusive that government efforts are far more likely to be the cause of the wealth gap than the solution.

This leads to one of the core facets of our problem: **Government doesn't**

produce anything. Anything it gives to one person or group, it must first take from someone else. It sucks capital out of the productive economy and uses it for activities that are largely unproductive.

The crisis we face is the inevitable result of the ways the government goes about taking the resources it has promised.

Let's use Detroit as an example...

In 1961, Detroit elected Democrat Jerome Cavanagh as mayor.

He won election by promising to give Detroit's African American population the civil rights they deserved. But Cavanagh didn't stop there. Seeing the political advantage of serving this community's interests, he did all he could to bring government benefits and government spending to Detroit's black community.

Mayor Cavanagh modeled development in Detroit after Soviet efforts to rebuild whole urban areas in Eastern Europe. The program attempted to turn a nine-square-mile section of the city (with 134,000 inhabitants) into a "Model City."

To help finance the effort, Cavanagh pushed a new income tax through the state legislature and a "commuter tax" on city workers. He promised the residents of the Model City... most of whom were poor and black... benefits that would be paid for by the rich. He bought the votes of the city's residents with taxes they didn't have to pay.

More than $400 million (almost $3 billion in today's dollars) was spent on the program. The feds and Democratic city mayors were soon telling people where to live, what to build, and what businesses to open or close. In return, the people received cash, training, education, and health care.

But they didn't like being told what to do or how to live. The Model City program was a disaster. Within five years, it had helped trigger a complete breakdown of civil order. The city's population began to rapidly decline.

On July 23, 1967, police attempted to break up a notorious after-hours club that featured gambling and prostitution in the heart of the new Model City. Many of these clubs had been in operation since Prohibition. The community tolerated these establishments – but the city's political leadership didn't want them in the new Model City area.

On this particular night, at this particular club, the community was celebrating the return of two Vietnam War veterans. More than 80 people had packed into the club. The police decided to arrest everyone present, including the two war vets. This outraged the entire neighborhood, which began to riot. The scene turned into the worst race riot of the 1960s.

The violence killed more than 40 people and left more than 5,000 people homeless. One of the first stores to be looted was a black-owned pharmacy. The largest black-owned clothing store in the city was also burned to the ground. Cavanagh did nothing to stop the riots. (He claimed a large police presence would make matters worse.) Five days later, President Johnson sent in two divisions of paratroopers to put down the violence.

The situation destabilized the entire city. Most of the people who could afford to leave did. Over the next 18 months, 140,000 upper- and middle-class residents – almost all of them white – left the city.

And so, you might ask... after five years of centralized planning, higher taxes, and a fleeing population... what did the government decide to do with its grand experiment?

It expanded the Model City program with 1974's Community Development Block Grant Program.

The subsequent failure of this program and many after it has decimated Detroit's economy and culture. Almost nothing is left of what was the capital of America's industrial heartland. Total vacant land in Detroit now occupies an area the size of Boston.

None of this is surprising. It's exactly what you'd expect to see given the implementation of a socialist scheme like the Model City program.

Always remember... **the government has to take resources from someone before it can dole them out to others.** This act of taking destroys an economy. The more you take from the productive members of society, the less productive they become. That's the primary lesson of the history of socialism. Yet many of our political leaders seem oblivious to this iron law of human nature.

So... how does the government go about taking the resources it has promised to distribute? The first and most obvious way – **taxes**.

You don't need me to tell you, our politicians have taken full advantage of their power to tax. But we're reaching their limits... Taxes can no longer be raised without people fleeing states. This has happened in several places – California, New Jersey, and New York, to name a few.

In Maryland – where my company is headquartered – the Democratic state government couldn't balance the budget in 2009, so it decided to double the income tax rate on citizens with more than $1 million in annual income. The editorial board at the *Baltimore Sun* newspaper happily praised the measure and predicted Maryland's top earners would "grin and bear it"... What a bunch of fools.

Instead, the rich left. The number of million-dollar incomes in the state of Maryland declined by more than 30%. Rather than gaining the predicted $106 million in income from these filers, Maryland collected $100 million *less* than it did the year before.

It's good politics to promise the voters that only the rich will pay.

Now take a look at the chart on the next page... You'll see that in 1950, the government only represented about 20% of our country's gross domestic product (GDP).

By 2014, that government slice was much bigger – 36%.

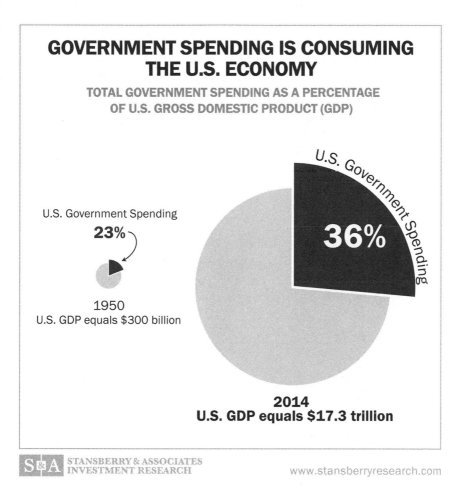

GOVERNMENT SPENDING IS CONSUMING THE U.S. ECONOMY

TOTAL GOVERNMENT SPENDING AS A PERCENTAGE OF U.S. GROSS DOMESTIC PRODUCT (GDP)

U.S. Government Spending
23%

1950
U.S. GDP equals $300 billion

U.S. Government Spending
36%

**2014
U.S. GDP equals $17.3 trillion**

S&A STANSBERRY & ASSOCIATES INVESTMENT RESEARCH

www.stansberryresearch.com

A huge portion of that pie comes directly from income taxes. But those taxes aren't evenly distributed across the whole country. The burden for an overwhelming amount of the taxes the government collects falls on just a few people.

In 2014, only 53% of the U.S. population paid federal income taxes.

And the top 25% of our country's earners paid nearly 90% of all income taxes collected.

This leads the 47% of Americans who didn't pay federal income taxes to believe the government doesn't cost them anything.

They are dead wrong.

Everyone is paying for the government whether they realize it or not. The 36%-plus of GDP that the government consumes comes out of everyone's pockets.

The tax revenue may come from the rich. But this capital would otherwise be used to start new businesses, create jobs, and invest in innovation.

Even those who do not pay taxes lose out on what would have been created by the existence of that money in the productive economy.

It also reduces the market's incentives for entrepreneurs. **The more you take from the productive members of society, the less productive they become.** That's the primary lesson of the history of socialism.

Chapter 2

The Corruption of Debt

Again, the only way government can give away something is by first taking it from someone else. This is critical. The government taking what it wants is exactly what has created the crisis we face.

Taxes are the most obvious way the government takes what it wants to redistribute. But as I said, our government is reaching the limits of what it can generate from new or higher taxes. When the government realizes it can't take any more from you through taxes, it uses debt to take from your children and grandchildren.

And our government has taken advantage of that option to a historic degree...

As of December 2014, the U.S. government owes roughly $18 trillion. The number is so large, it's meaningless. No one can comprehend how much money $18 trillion really is. A better way to think about it is each American taxpayer owes roughly $153,000. That's like a whole additional mortgage for most people.

A 2014 Harvard study put it in this way:

> If the federal government spent its yearly revenues exclusively on debt reduction and ceased all of its operations, it would take three of four years to pay down the debt. Or, the government could pay down the debt in one blow if it simply took more than $52,000 from every person living in the U.S., including children, the elderly, and the unemployed. If this one-time "debt reduction fee" were levied only on those in the workforce, the cost would be over $106,000 per person.

And it's not just the federal government that has become addicted to debt. If you add up all of our government, corporate, and consumer debt, America owes roughly $60 trillion.

As the next chart shows... that adds up to about $730,000 per American household.

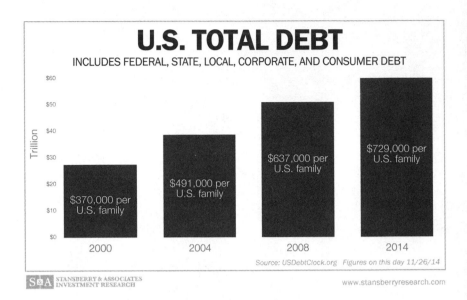

This massive amount of national debt cannot be financed at any real rate of interest.

If the government had to pay even 6% interest on its debt, it would cost nearly $1 trillion a year. And that's just to pay the interest on the debt. The entire government brings in less than $3 trillion a year in taxes.

The next chart shows what would happen in that scenario...

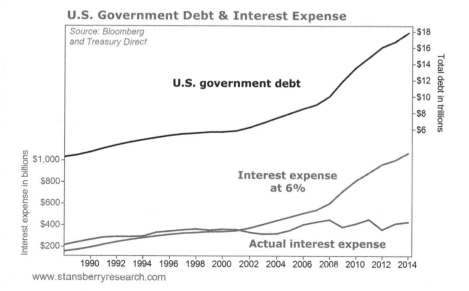

U.S. Government Debt & Interest Expense

Source: Bloomberg and Treasury Direct

www.stansberryresearch.com

This debt addiction has filtered into three critical areas of the economy. Instead of learning from the mistakes that crippled our economy in 2009 when the mortgage bubble burst, we have created three new bubbles that could soon blow up...

The largest threat is the U.S. corporate bond market, particularly junk bonds.

When this crash occurs, it will be the largest destruction of wealth in history. There has never been a bigger bubble in U.S. bonds.

How do I know? It's simple. Historically, junk bonds (aka high-yield bonds issued by less creditworthy companies) have never yielded less than 5% annually. But they hit that low in mid-2014, and by the end of the year were up to a bit more than 6%.

Likewise, the difference between the yields on junk bonds and the yields on investment-grade bonds has almost never been smaller. That means credit is more available today than almost ever before for small, less-than-investment-grade firms. The last time credit was this widely available – and at such low costs – was in 2007. And that ended badly.

The coming collapse in the bond market will be far worse than it was last time, too. The Federal Reserve's twin policies of keeping interest rates near zero and buying tens of billions of dollars in Treasury securities and mortgage-backed debt have driven the huge bull market in bonds. As the Fed buys bonds, it pushes bond rates down and forces the other buyers of bonds to buy riskier debt that historically offers much higher yields.

I believe we'll see a real panic in the corporate bond market at some point soon. I expect the average price of non-investment-grade debt (aka junk bonds) to fall 50%. Investment-grade bonds will fall substantially, too. (I'd estimate something around 25%.) This is going to wipe out a huge amount of capital... and believe me... it's almost 100% guaranteed to happen.

Junk-bond guru Martin Fridson has projected $1.6 trillion of bonds and loans will begin to default in 2016. That means three times as many debt issuers will default than the last recession.

This would have already happened, according to Fridson, but the government has kept interest rates artificially low, making it possible for many at-risk debt-issuers to refinance their debt at a lower interest rate. This delayed an inevitable wave of defaults in the junk-bond industry, but only temporarily. But the government cannot keep interest rates low forever...

Meanwhile, **student debt is forming another looming bubble.** As of 2014, student debt totals more than **$1 trillion.**

The average college student now graduates with $24,000 in debt... and by his late 20s has racked up more than $6,000 in credit card debt. Meanwhile, median earnings for Americans aged 25-34 equals $34,000-$38,000.

Can you imagine starting out your adult life with a personal debt-to-income level at close to 100%? What does this say about the state of our economy? What does this say about the state of our culture?

All the signs show that the debt piled on our youth will become another catastrophic bubble in the American economy.

Bloomberg financial news and data service reported that default in this sector in 2014 is at its absolute highest since 1995. And Jim Rickards, the author of *Currency Wars*, calls the student debt market the "next subprime crisis."

According to the Wall Street Journal, **33%** of student loans are held by subprime borrowers – the riskiest folks.

What does it say about our economy when the youth have become saddled with so much debt that one-third of college graduates will likely default on their loans?

America's youth aren't the only ones who have acquired a mountain of debt in the last few years.

The third subprime lending bubble poised to cripple the economy is the automotive sector. Most people have no idea how pervasive subprime loans have become in auto lending.

As with mortgage lending, car lending used to be a simple and safe business. Local and regional banks (or finance companies) would provide loans to customers with good credit and a substantial down payment.

The term of the loan didn't exceed the useful life of the car. Under these conditions, auto loans were extremely low-risk. Losses on auto loans have historically been extremely low – less than 2%. Auto loans even performed well in the Great Depression.

Then things got out of control in 2011, after Wall Street firms started buying up auto-lending groups. They changed the terms: extending auto loans up to 84 months (seven years), lowering the down payments (on leases they're next to nothing), and radically lowering the credit scores required to qualify.

Now, more people than ever before are borrowing money to buy cars. As of 2013, Americans owe $783 billion against their cars and trucks. *Unbelievably, 34% of this debt is now owed by subprime credits.*

We've also seen a big uptick in the amount of subprime auto loans that are being securitized and sold to other investors. These securitizations move credit risk away from the car companies and finance companies and onto investors – the same thing that happened in the housing bubble.

As we know from the recent housing bust... when subprime lending goes too far and becomes too large a percentage of total lending, it can cause overall credit quality to collapse. In the car business, that could cause huge problems going forward, problems big enough to harm our entire economy.

This debt will create a depression that will be worse than it was in 2008. This time, the government has allowed massive amounts of debt to be piled on the weakest in our society... namely, our country's youth. When this bubble breaks, it will be an entire generation of young Americans who will suffer.

When these three bubbles pop, the consequences will be dire for many people. But remember, they are symptoms of a deeper problem... our economy and our culture have become addicted to debt. The sense of entitlement that has developed in our culture tells people they are "owed" things they cannot afford... and our government is leading by example and piling on debts to pay for things we cannot afford.

The United States has become the largest debtor in human history. It's disgusting that we would leave a burden like this for our children and grandchildren...

And it also opens the door to the final corruption of America...

As I explained, ignore for a moment how impossible it is for us to pay off the debts we have accumulated. We are fast approaching the point where the government cannot even afford to pay the interest on the debt.

And that leaves it with one last tool to perpetuate its power...

Chapter 3

The Corruption of Currency

When the government taps out its ability to increase its tax revenue and its debts become too mountainous to maintain... it has one last way it can take what it needs. And it may be the most insidious.

It can print the dollars it needs to pay for what it wants.

This is a relatively new phenomenon for the U.S. government. Throughout most of our history, one thing kept our government from printing all the dollars it wanted – gold. Until the mid-20th century, the dollar represented an explicit promise. It represented one small claim on the U.S. government's gold reserve. And the size of the reserve limited the dollars available for circulation.

But in 1971, Nixon severed the U.S. dollar's last tie to gold. From then on, we were free to take on as much debt as the world would lend us... and print as much money as we needed to finance it.

Since the 2008-2009 financial crisis, the Federal Reserve has largely kept the printing presses running full-tilt. Its quantitative easing policies (printing billions of dollars and using them to buy Treasury securities and mortgage-backed debt) have caused the volume of currency to balloon.

The Federal Reserve's balance sheet – which represents the total amount of currency in circulation or in a central bank's reserves – has blown up from $1.1 trillion in 2008 to $4 trillion in 2014.

Federal Reserve Monetary Base

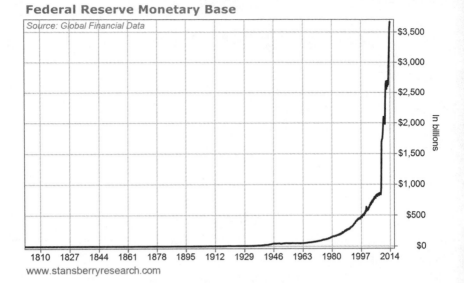

Source: Global Financial Data

www.stansberryresearch.com

Not many people understand the fallacy of these actions or their inevitable failure. The great advantage of paper money is supposed to be its flexibility. You can, in theory, print more of it when you need it to facilitate economic growth or forestall a crisis. But it doesn't really work.

Printing money doesn't create wealth or stimulate the economy. Instead, it simply makes each dollar less valuable and leads to higher prices, a monetary phenomenon we call "inflation."

It is an insidious form of stealing. People feel wealthier as the numbers on their paychecks and bank balances rise. As nominal stock prices rise, people feel as though things are going well. But they don't notice the value of those dollars is eroding steadily.

Worse, it provides incentives for going into debt. People who borrowed today will repay those obligations in the future with dollars that are worth much less...

Inflation has been so prevalent for so long, most people don't even know it's not part of a normal economic system. Data on consumer prices from 1596-1971 in Britain prove that during gold-standard periods, commodity prices remain level – even over hundreds of years, during periods of massive economic growth and soaring populations.

The most important test of paper money is whether it facilitates real, per-capita economic growth. And on that score, the evidence is overwhelmingly negative. Measured in ounces of gold, per-family income in the United States has declined since 1971, retreating back to 1950s levels, despite the advent of two-income families.

Measured another way (using the government's own consumer price index as the inflation adjustment), real per-family income is essentially unchanged since 1971, again despite the fact that far more households have two wage earners today. Household earnings, in real terms, have fallen 30%-50% since the gold standard was abandoned.

Paper money works great for the rich, who can hedge their exposure to the currency and whose access to fixed-rate credit allows huge asset purchases. But it is horrible for the middle class, whose wages do not keep pace with declines in purchasing power caused by inflation. If you want to know why there's so much discrepancy in incomes and per-capita wealth in the U.S., look no further than paper money.

Any reasonable study of paper-money systems versus gold-backed monetary systems demonstrates the superiority of gold immediately. So... why does almost every modern government choose paper? The answer is because paper money allows the wealthy and powerful vested interests in our economy to manipulate interest rates, prices, the money supply, and credit to their exclusive advantage.

Think about this for a second. Imagine how much productivity in our economy has increased since 1971. There's been a complete revolution in technology that has caused huge increases to productivity. You can see it all around you. I'd estimate productivity has increased by 4%-6% per year since 1971.

Where did all that wealth go? It didn't end up boosting the value of our currency, as you'd expect. Prices never fell. Instead, all those productivity gains were consumed by the issuance of more and more money – by inflation.

Therefore, average wages, in real terms, have declined. And all these productivity gains – all that wealth – was consumed by the financial sector, the government, debtors... all the people who benefit from inflation.

As you can see in this chart, based on one originally published by the Economic Policy Institute think tank... when we took the dollar off gold and allowed the central bank to continuously debase the currency, the dollar and the wages paid in the dollar no longer kept pace with inflation.

Thus, when trade or innovation leads to a gain in productivity (and the loss of a job), there is no reciprocal benefit to wages for the middle class. The replacement job is sure to come at a much lower real wage.

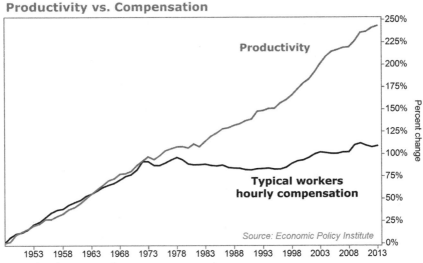

Productivity vs. Compensation

Source: Economic Policy Institute

www.stansberryresearch.com

As a result, we've been left with a heavily indebted economy that's still led by consumption. Our system rewards debtors and punishes savers. It makes long-term capital investment nearly impossible because of economic volatility and financial risks caused by inflation. Worst of all, our system requires everyone become a speculator because there's no other way to safeguard savings.

What the gold standard really does is ensure a level playing field for all economic actors – borrowers, lenders, and even governments. That's why bankers (who are always highly leveraged), media barons (who constantly borrow to buy more properties), and governments (which can never balance their budgets) all abhor gold. To maintain their power, they all need paper money. The system we have now and those who profit from it would not survive a transition back to the gold standard.

The little-known reality of our paper money system is that it robs our currency of gains to purchasing power. That means the average person is working harder, producing more, but cannot buy as much as they used to. Meanwhile, asset prices have soared. The wealthy become wealthier as the value of everything they own becomes inflated along with our currency. This explains why the wealth gap has grown so much since 2000.

And it explains why the wealth gap will continue to grow, so long as our government continues its corrupt policies of quantitative easing, corporate bailouts, overspending, and over-taxing.

These policies accomplish nothing other than making the rich richer, the poor poorer, and destroying the world's faith in the U.S. dollar...

But our paper money does one other thing that I believe could ultimately bring about its own demise... It steals from our creditors.

As I've explained, borrowers today will repay their debts in devalued dollars. That's a bad deal for lenders. And as I've said, at this point, America is dependent on its lenders to sustain our standard of living.

However, I believe governments and entities around the world that hold U.S. debt have grown tired of watching the value of those obligations inflated away. And I believe we're facing a mutiny on the dollar.

— Chapter 4 —

The Mutiny on the Dollar

For many years now, it's been clear that China would soon be pulling the strings in the U.S. financial system.

After all, the American people now owe the Chinese government nearly $1.5 trillion. Big numbers don't mean much to most people, but keep in mind... this tab is now hundreds of billions of dollars more than what the U.S. government collects in ALL income taxes (both corporate and individual) each year. It's basically a sum we can never, ever hope to repay – at least, not by normal means.

Of course, the Chinese aren't stupid. They realize we are both trapped. We are stuck with an enormous debt we can never realistically repay... and the Chinese are trapped with an outstanding loan they can neither get rid of nor hope to collect. So the Chinese government is now taking a radical approach.

China is now engaged in a full-fledged currency war with the United States. The ultimate goal – as the Chinese have publicly stated – is to create a new dominant world currency, dislodge the U.S. dollar from its current reserve role, and recover as much of the $1.5 trillion the U.S. government has borrowed as possible.

The Chinese need to do a couple things to make their yuan (also called the renminbi) a global currency. First, they have to establish bilateral trading agreements with various countries around the world. Currently, all international trade is done in dollars.

These bilateral agreements mean trade can clear in China's own currency, bypassing the dollar. So in other words, you have to find people who are willing to hold the yuan instead of holding the dollar. And the following chart shows how the yuan-denominated trade grew from 2012 to 2014...

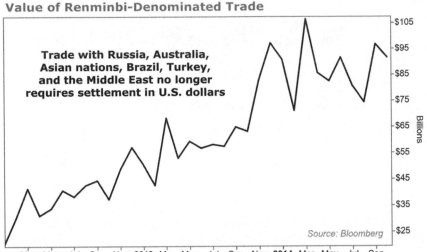

Value of Renminbi-Denominated Trade

Trade with Russia, Australia, Asian nations, Brazil, Turkey, and the Middle East no longer requires settlement in U.S. dollars

Source: Bloomberg

Mar May Jul Sep Nov **2013** Mar May Jul Sep Nov **2014** Mar May Jul Sep

www.stansberryresearch.com

Next thing China has to do is make its yuan the currency of choice for debt. And we're seeing that happen, too. Turned off by super-low interest rates and constant money printing, entrepreneurs and investors are starting to turn away from the dollar. They're looking for stability in a new kind of financial product called the "dim sum" bond. That's simply a regular bond denominated in Chinese currency.

This next chart represents the single biggest threat to your wealth. It represents the growth in issuance of dim sum bonds. The volumes are still low, but they're growing rapidly. It won't be long before more corporate debt is issued in yuan than in the dollar... And when that happens, that's the end. The dollar will not come back.

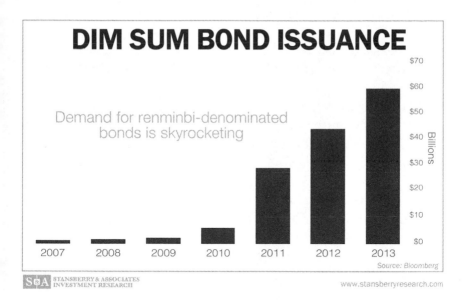

The final thing that the Chinese are going to do to establish their currency as the world's reserve is simple. They're going to back it with gold...

China has made gold ownership legal for individuals. But it does not allow any exports of gold. And it's mining huge volumes of it. You can see that in this chart of its production figures...

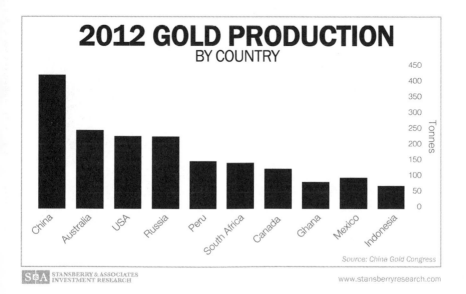

China's gold holdings are still not nearly as large as ours, but it's catching up. It's producing more than anybody else in the world by a large margin. It's reinvesting about 90% of its trade surpluses into gold holdings. You can see that by looking at the Chinese gold coming in through Hong Kong.

The Chinese are slowly hedging their exposure to the dollar by becoming the world's leading gold investor. By building a huge stockpile of gold, they will be able to back their currency with the world's traditional form of money.

Once they make the yuan freely convertible to gold, they will have created tremendous demand for their bonds and bills by making their currency the world's most reliable.

The impact on the dollar will be catastrophic...

PART TWO

The Future of America

— Chapter 1 —

This Is Why There Are No Jobs in America

Below is an essay I first published in November 2009. This piece is unusual and controversial... But it remains the best insight into the United States' sluggish economy and unemployment situation you'll read today.

I'd like to make you a business offer.

Seriously. This is a real offer. In fact, you really can't turn me down, as you'll come to understand in a moment...

Here's the deal. You're going to start a business or expand the one you've got now. It doesn't really matter what you do or what you're going to do. I'll partner with you no matter what business you're in – as long as it's legal.

But I can't give you any capital – you have to come up with that on your own. I won't give you any labor – that's definitely up to you. What I will do, however, is demand you follow all sorts of rules about what products and services you can offer, how much (and how often) you pay your employees, and where and when you're allowed to operate your business. That's my role in the affair – to tell you what to do.

Now in return for my rules, I'm going to take roughly half of whatever you make in the business each year. Half seems fair, doesn't it? I think so. Of course, that's half of your profits.

You're also going to have to pay me about 12% of whatever you decide to pay your employees because you've got to cover my expenses for promulgating all the rules about who you can employ, when, where, and how. Come on, you're my partner. It's only "fair."

25

Now… after you've put your hard-earned savings at risk to start this business, and after you've worked hard at it for a few decades (paying me my 50% or a bit more along the way each year), you might decide you'd like to cash out – to finally live the good life.

Whether or not this is "fair" – some people never can afford to retire – is a different argument. As your partner, I'm happy for you to sell whenever you'd like… because our agreement says, if you sell, you have to pay me an additional 20% of whatever the capitalized value of the business is at that time.

I know… I know… you put up all the original capital. You took all the risks. You put in all the labor. That's all true. But I've done my part, too. I've collected 50% of the profits each year. And I've always come up with more rules for you to follow each year. Therefore, I deserve another, final 20% slice of the business.

Oh… and one more thing…

Even after you've sold the business and paid all of my fees… I'd recommend buying lots of life insurance. You see, even after you've been retired for years, when you die, you'll have to pay me 50% of whatever your estate is worth.

After all, I've got lots of partners and not all of them are as successful as you and your family. We don't think it's "fair" for your kids to have such a big advantage. But if you buy enough life insurance, you can finance this expense for your children.

All in all, if you're a very successful entrepreneur… if you're one of the rare, lucky, and hard-working people who can create a new company, employ lots of people, and satisfy the public… you'll end up paying me more than 75% of your income over your life. Thanks so much.

I'm sure you'll think my offer is reasonable and happily partner with me… But it doesn't really matter how you feel about it because if you ever try to stiff me – or cheat me on any of my fees or rules – I'll break down your door in the middle of the night, threaten you and your family with heavy, automatic weapons, and throw you in jail.

That's how civil society is supposed to work, right? This is Amerika, isn't it?

That's the offer Amerika gives its entrepreneurs. And the idiots in Washington wonder why there are no new jobs...

Chapter 2

USA: The Next Detroit

Detroit's history of socialist experiments has laid waste to what was once among America's most vibrant metropolises.

I see these same problems that destroyed Detroit as a clear analogy to the problems that are eroding American society… its economic standing in the world… its reputation for innovation and productivity… and the standard of living that generations of Americans have assumed is our birthright.

One of the most important things to remember about socialism – or coercion of any kind – is it fails eventually because human beings have an innate desire for liberty and a strong need for personal property rights.

In fact, the origins of government lie in the need of agricultural communities to protect themselves from violence and theft. So it is particularly ironic that in more recent times, it is government itself that has more frequently played the role of bandit.

When you start taxing people at extreme rates to pay for socialist "benefits," when you start telling them which schools their children must attend, when you start giving jobs away to people based on race instead of ability… you quash human freedom, which bogs down productivity, and if continued for long enough, leads to social collapse.

I find it perplexing that only 20 years after the collapse of the Berlin Wall, the West continues to implement laws that mimic all of the failed policies of our former "communist" foes. President Obama won the election by promising to "spread the wealth around."

But truth be told… we don't have to look to Eastern Europe or the Soviet Union to find a society destroyed by coercion, socialism, and the overreaching power of the State. We could just look at Detroit…

In 1961, the last Republican mayor of Detroit lost his re-election bid to a young, intelligent Democrat, with the overwhelming support of newly organized black voters. His name was Jerome Cavanagh. The incumbent was widely considered to be corrupt (and later served 10 years in prison for tax evasion). Cavanagh, a white man, pandered to poor underclass black voters.

He marched with Martin Luther King down the streets of Detroit in 1963. (Of course, marching with King was the right thing to do... It's just Cavanagh's motives were political, not moral.)

He instated aggressive affirmative action policies at City Hall. And most critically, he greatly expanded the role of the government in Detroit, taking advantage of President Lyndon Johnson's "Model Cities Program" – the first great experiment in centralized urban planning.

Mayor Cavanagh was the only elected official to serve on Johnson's task force. And Detroit received widespread acclaim for its leadership in the program, which attempted to turn a nine-square-mile section of the city (with 134,000 inhabitants) into a "model city." More than $400 million was spent trying to turn inner cities into shining new monuments to government planning.

In short, the feds and Democratic city mayors were soon telling people where to live, what to build, and what businesses to open or close. In return, the people received cash, training, education, and health care.

The Model Cities program was a disaster for Detroit. But it did accomplish its real goal: The creation of a state-supported, Democratic political power base. The program also resulted in much higher taxes – which were easy to pitch to poor voters who didn't have to pay them. Cavanagh pushed a new income tax through the state legislature and a "commuter tax" on city workers.

Unfortunately, as with all socialist programs, lots of folks simply don't like being told what to do. Lots of folks don't like being plundered by the government. They don't like losing their jobs because of their race.

In Detroit, they didn't like paying new, large taxes to fund a largely black and Democratic political hegemony. And so in 1966, more than 22,000 middle- and upper-class residents moved out of the city.

But what about the poor? As my friend Doug Casey likes to say, in the War on Poverty, the poor lost the most. In July 1967, police attempted to break up a late-night party in the middle of the new "Model City." The scene turned into the worst race riot of the 1960s. The violence killed more than 40 people and left more than 5,000 people homeless. One of the first stores to be looted was the black-owned pharmacy.

The largest black-owned clothing store in the city was also burned to the ground. Cavanagh did nothing to stop the riots, fearing a large police presence would make matters worse. Five days later, Johnson sent in two divisions of paratroopers to put down the insurrection. Over the next 18 months, an additional 140,000 upper- and middle-class residents – almost all of them white – left the city.

And so, you might rightfully ask... after five years of centralized planning, higher taxes, and a fleeing population, what did the government decide to do with its grand experiment, its "Model City"? You'll never guess...

Seeing it had accomplished nothing but failure, the government endeavored to do still more. The Model City program was expanded and enlarged by 1974's Community Development Block Grant Program. Here again, politicians would decide which groups (and even individuals) would receive state funds for various "renewal" schemes.

Later, Big Business was brought into the fold. In exchange for various concessions, the Big Three automakers "gave" $488 million to the city for use in still more redevelopment schemes in the mid-1990s.

What happened? Even with all their power and money, centralized planners couldn't succeed with any of their plans. Nearly all the upper and middle classes left Detroit. The poor fled, too. The Model City area lost 63% of its population and 45% of its housing units from the inception of the program through 1990.

The crisis continues. At an auction of nearly 9,000 seized homes and lots, less than one-fifth of the available properties sold, even with bidding starting at $500. You literally can't give away most of the "Model City" areas.

Total vacant land in Detroit occupies an area the size of Boston. Detroit properties in foreclosure have more than tripled since 2007.

Every single mayor of Detroit since 1961 has been a Democrat. Every single mayor of Detroit since 1974 has been black. Detroit has been a major recipient of every major social program since the early 1960s and has received hundreds of billions of dollars in government grants, loans, and programs. We now have a black, Democrat president, who is promising to do to America as a whole what his political mentors have done to Detroit.

Those of you with a Democratic political affiliation may think what I've written above is biased or false. You may think what you like. But there is no way to argue that what the government has done to Detroit is anything but a horrendous crime.

You may think what I've written above is merely a political analysis. Perhaps so, but politicians drive macroeconomic policy. And macroeconomic policy determines key financial metrics, like the trade-weighted value of a currency and key interest rates.

The likelihood America will become a giant Detroit is growing – rapidly. Politicians now control the banking sector, most of the manufacturing sector (including autos), a large amount of media, and are threatening to take over health care and the production of electricity (via cap and trade rules).

These are the biggest threats to wealth in the history of our country. And these threats are causing the world's most accomplished and wealthy investors to actively short-sell the United States – something that is unprecedented in my experience.

— Chapter 3 —

It Can Always Get Worse

If you think things in Detroit can't deteriorate any further... The owners of the Penobscot Building there have a warning for you...

The Penobscot Building is a hallmark of downtown Detroit.

It was built in 1928. At 47 stories, it was the eighth-tallest building *anywhere* in the world when it was completed. It was the absolute tallest building anywhere in the world outside of Chicago and New York. It remained the tallest building in Michigan for almost 50 years.

It's much more than merely a local landmark. It is Detroit's trademark tower. The landlord lights the tower at night to celebrate Christmas and Independence Day. The building is ornate and beautiful, done in an art-deco style reminiscent of Rockefeller Center in New York.

Yes... two other buildings in Detroit are now taller, bigger, and newer... but the Penobscot Building is still, even after all these years, considered Class-A commercial space. She's the grand dame.

Buildings like Penobscot would cost hundreds of dollars per square foot to build... perhaps even $1,000 a square foot, considering all the ornate stone work on the exterior. That's not including the value of the land where the building sits – square in the middle of Detroit's financial center.

We all know commercial real estate hasn't done much in terms of price appreciation since the crash of 2008. Class-A commercial space like this sold for around $200 per square foot, on average, in 2013. At that same time, my company was in negotiations to buy an office building in Delray Beach, Florida for around $240 per square foot. At 776,000 square feet, a building like Penobscot, in good condition, might cost $150 million-$200 million to buy, on average, in cities across the U.S.

Unfortunately for the previous owners, Detroit isn't anyone's idea of a great place to start a business or to move headquarters. *Class-A commercial real estate in Detroit traded around $28 per square foot in 2012.* That's roughly 86% less than the national average... and probably 90% less than new construction.

While owners are not *technically* giving these properties away (at least not yet), these prices indicate the city has suffered a total collapse. Surely things can't get any worse, right?

That's exactly what many investors thought back in 2007, too. And I admit... I was one of them. In fact, I asked my analyst Tom Dyson to spend some time in Detroit. I wanted him to find a few different ways for our subscribers to buy assets there.

After spending a few weeks in Detroit, Tom came back with lots of good ideas. One was to buy the skyscrapers, which were selling at the cheapest prices available anywhere in the world.

Why on Earth was I interested in Detroit?

I wasn't naïve. I knew a lot about the city's history. I've probably written as much about Detroit's woes as just about any financial analyst. I've long believed that Detroit is a kind of petri dish... a place where various ideas about how governments and societies ought to be organized were tested.

Anyone who's spent any time studying the outcome of socialist societies or the real impact of unions on an industry won't be surprised by the outcome. Detroit lost 80% of its population and nearly all of its working and middle classes in the "Model city" movement we discussed earlier. What was left was the poorest, most violent city in America.

I believe it's a warning to all of us... about what might happen if we continue down the path we're on today. Anyone who believes more debt, taxes, and government will save our economy and lead us to prosperity ought to move to Detroit for a year. Let me know how it turns out.

In any case, the point I'm trying to make is... I wasn't ignorant of the risks Detroit posed. I simply figured things *couldn't possibly* get any worse.

As early as March 14, 2007, I was predicting that a GM bankruptcy filing was inevitable. With the stock then trading around $40 per share, my call was so far outside the consensus, many subscribers thought I was out of my mind...

Yes, I thought it was likely that Chrysler would go under too, as its balance sheet was in the same poor shape. Ford was different, only because it had borrowed a huge chunk of cash in 2006, money that did, in fact, see it through the crisis.

So... why was I bullish on Detroit real estate in 2007 if I was expecting a GM bankruptcy?

A real bankruptcy of GM – a true liquidation of the company's assets and a restructuring of its liabilities – would have transformed Detroit into one of the most vibrant and fastest-growing cities in the world. I was even looking to buy a house there. Yes, really.

You have to imagine what might have been...

Imagine what would have happened if the company's pension obligations had been discharged through the bankruptcy process. Imagine if all the real estate, all the machines... all the brands... and all the employees... would have been set free from the corrupt regime that's been slowly strangling them for decades.

Believe me, the people of Michigan can build cars that are just as good as the Germans and just as cost-effective as folks in Tennessee and South Carolina. The differences between GM's operations in Michigan and BMW's in South Carolina come down to legacy costs (pensions) and union rules.

When the local economy has to support a union-enforced "jobs bank" – where employees are literally paid to sit in a cafeteria all day – the local economy is doomed.

That's not just because of the lost productivity and the expense of paying those 10,000 folks. It's because of what a "job bank" communicates. It's a constant message of hopelessness, futility, and dependency. These ideas, expenses, and hopelessness have been dogging Michigan for almost 30 years.

But bad ideas don't last forever...

I assumed the failure of GM would wipe away this stain. Surely GM's assets would be auctioned off to the highest bidder. Surely the pensions would be restructured, the insane job banks destroyed. And the union rules gutted.

Call me a heartless capitalist if you must... but then explain under what other set of conditions could 70,000 employees at GM be expected to care for the 700,000 retirees depending on them? (Yes, those are the real numbers.)

If GM's managers were to have any hope of honoring even a part of the commitment the company owed to its retired workers, the existing employees would have to be free to work in the most efficient ways. They'd have to become some of the most productive workers anywhere in the world.

You don't find those kinds of people sitting in a jobs bank.

Post-bankruptcy... the entire culture in Detroit might have changed. It has happened before in many different industries that failed after decades of union oppression. Witness the transformation of the U.S. steel industry after the industry collapsed in the late 1990s.

But that's not what happened in Detroit.

Rather than letting the free market take its course, the U.S. government refused to allow the existing bankruptcy laws to shape the outcome. Instead, the president (Barack Obama) appointed one of the most corrupt political operatives in America – Steve Rattner, who was under investigation at the time for bribing state pension officials in New York – to oversee a "reorganization." His real job was to deliver still more power to the unions who'd help re-elect Obama. And sadly, that's what he did.

The government and the bondholders both had about $50 billion invested in GM. So after the bankruptcy and restructuring, it was surprising to find that the union was awarded 40% of the restructured company's equity, wiping out about 80% of the bondholder's claims. Worse, nothing... not one thing... was done to address the company's soaring pension obligations.

And so... what do you think the outcome has been?

When union rules, unlimited medical obligations, and pensions have destroyed in one of the greatest industrial corporations in American history... what do you think will happen when you leave the union with 40% of the restructured entity and take away none of its power and pension claims?

Former GM President Charles Erwin Wilson is famously quoted as saying, "What's good for GM is good for America."

But the inverse is certainly true, too. *What's bad for GM is also bad for America.* By postponing the liquidation of GM's assets and preventing a genuine restructuring of its obligations, our political leaders and their union backers have condemned Detroit's economy to still more decline – perhaps additional decades of decline.

You can see this by looking at the local real estate. Rather than rebounding after GM's government-led bailout, Detroit's commercial real estate sector has continued to collapse.

Take the Penobscot Building I mentioned earlier. It was bought in 2005 for $14 million, or about $18 per square foot. It seemed like an incredible deal at the time. But in 2013, the building sold again after a long, drawn-out bankruptcy proceeding.

The buyer, a Toronto-based real estate company, paid $5 million. That's $6.44 per square foot, a 64% decline since only 2005. And to us, 2005 looked like the bottom. As unpleasant as it is to imagine, things can certainly get worse.

What should we do about it?

The ultimate endgame to this crisis will be a massive collapse in the global monetary system. We're not there yet. You've still got time to buy real assets like gold, real estate, agricultural real estate, timber, and oil and gas reserves.

You've got time to buy certain kinds of operating companies that tend to prosper during periods of inflation – businesses like insurance companies.

These kinds of investments will survive the ongoing global currency "reset."

But the one key thing to remember is, while there will be lots of volatility (lots of ups and downs), this crisis won't go away until the debts are handled. And as we've seen with GM, the political class will do almost everything but deal with the root of these problems.

That means these problems won't be solved for a long, long time. And I believe... despite the low yields we're looking at in the Treasury... despite the huge run we've seen in gold and silver... that things will still get a lot worse in the real economy before they get better.

Chapter 4

The Future of America

As I look around at the world economy, I see two dominant trends.

First, major Western economies are impoverished by their debts and are struggling to avoid a collapse via desperate attempts to print their way out of perdition.

Second, I see the rise of the world's largest future economy in the midst of a massive effort to buy gold and control the global market.

The future will be dominated by surges in economic activity around the world, on the heels of massive monetary stimulus.

America is at a turning point unlike anything our country has ever experienced.

Like I said, I am an optimist, and believe our country will eventually take actions to right the catastrophic imbalance that threatens to collapse our country, our morality, and our culture.

But I wonder if I am too optimistic... Will we be able to create necessary change before it's too late?

Can we help educate our friends, family, and neighbors of the parasitic values that plague our nation?

Will we right the wrongs of the last 50 years... restore dignity, morality, and independence to our country?

I cannot answer these questions... I alone cannot fix our nation's problems.

That's why I – along with a team of brilliant financial minds, researchers, and industry experts – have spent so much time and energy putting together the ideas in this book. We have pulled together the absolute most important ideas and recommendations that are essential for every American to know.

And with this book as your aid, you will have all the necessary tools to survive and prosper during the desperate years America has in store.

PART THREE

The Three Assets You Do NOT Have to Report to the U.S. Government

How to Prepare for the Biggest Government Encroachment in U.S. History

Things may seem OK on the surface in America.

By and large, the neighborhood you woke up in today feels a lot like it always did.

Your friends still tool around in the same kinds of cars they always did. You and your wife still go for dinner and a movie when you can find a babysitter. And you still go over to your neighbor's house on Saturday to drink a couple beers and watch the game on his big-screen TV.

But I can tell you with near certainty that the next few years are going to be a major shock for most people in this country.

The debts our country has rung up are coming due, and we can't afford them anymore... Literally, we cannot afford the interest payments on our national debt.

We're on the cusp of a disaster...

It will result in the biggest government encroachment in our country's history. It's coming hard... and fast. And most people are going to be totally unprepared for the consequences.

I'm talking about much higher taxes. I'm talking about currency controls. I'm talking about the loss of personal freedoms we have taken for granted for more than 100 years.

The only good news in this is that it's not too late for you to do something about it.

That's why I encourage everyone I know to take a few simple steps now to protect your money and your family.

And that's what I'm going to show you how to do in this section... It's the No. 1 thing you need to do to protect and grow your wealth.

The Time to Protect Yourself Is Now

Maybe you're content to think heavy taxes aren't your problem... that if a few rich folks feel the pinch, well... what's it to you?

If that's what you think... you're wrong.

As my friend, colleague, and *Retirement Millionaire* editor Dr. David Eifrig wrote in 2009...

> Without belaboring the point, it's unimaginable that the U.S. can pay off its debts in our lifetimes... But here's the catch – it's going to try... Or rather pretend to try. And the only way to do that is to tax the beejeezus out of anyone with a few assets to his name.
>
> Look, this is not a problem just for the wealthy. This is for anyone with a lifetime of savings. Under the current path, everyone who has something will be forced to give it up to those who don't have anything. And worse, we'll be forced to give it to those too lazy to work for anything. I don't know about you, but first and foremost, I want to decide whom my money goes to. I don't want some bureaucrat in D.C. telling me how kind I have to be.

The way to protect yourself from runaway government thievery is to diversify your assets offshore... to move some portion of your wealth out of the country, somewhere safe.

And the time to protect yourself is now... before the government restricts the flow of currency in and out of the country... before it outlaws your ability to move you and your assets around... before it starts confiscating things like gold. (Don't laugh, FDR did it.)

I realize pulling up stakes and heading to an offshore "safe haven" isn't realistic for everyone. But that doesn't mean you're trapped, that you have to accept whatever the government has in store...

Several of the editors at Stansberry Research and I have been investigating how to do this legally. ("Legally" is critical... Remember, we're talking about this because we don't want to jeopardize our freedom.)

Below, you'll find a few key steps Dr. Eifrig advises you take without uprooting yourself. It's some of the most sensible, nuts-and-bolts advice I've read on the subject. I'm republishing his research in this book because everyone with a few assets to protect should take these three steps... at least.

And last, before we get started, you need one other piece of advice: **Keep this to yourself.** All of Dr. Eifrig's tips are perfectly legal. But as he says, "That doesn't mean the government *wants* you to do these things... To the contrary, if too many people start talking about these things and taking these steps, the government could easily change the rules."

Three Tips to Keep Your Wealth Out of the United States

By Dr. David Eifrig

TIP No. 1: Open a Foreign Bank Account – Soon

If you open up a foreign financial account with less than $10,000, you do not have to report the assets. This comes under the Foreign Bank and Financial Authority (FBAR) regulations, and the IRS states you only have to report if:

- You have financial interest in, signature authority, or other authority over one or more accounts in a foreign country.

- The aggregate value of all foreign financial accounts exceeds $10,000 at any time during the calendar year.

If you keep more than $10,000 in total overseas, you must report it or risk fines and jail time. (A mere 50% of your assets and up to five years in prison, if a judge decides the oversight was willful.)

Be careful about interest-earning accounts, too. Let's say you put $9,990 in an account in January and you earn enough interest to take you to more than $10,000 by year end. Well, guess what? Now, you must report the assets and the income.

And make sure you open a holding account... This allows you to keep the account in the currency of your choice.

One more secret: Nothing prevents your spouse and other family members from doing the same. A family of six could keep about $59,000 in accounts overseas and not need to report it. Again, this is all legal and a great way to diversify your portfolio around the world.

There's one foreign bank in which you can easily open an account online – no visit required. The bank is Caye International Bank Limited (CIBL) in Belize.

You've probably never heard of CIBL, and that's because foreign banks are not allowed to advertise in the U.S. the same way domestic banks can. But trust me when I tell you Caye Bank is safer than most U.S. banks.

You see, Belize mandates its banks maintain 24% capital liquidity versus the 3%-10% in the U.S. In other words, your bank in Belize has cash to cover 24% of the demand deposits it carries. They don't make banks much more liquid than this.

Anyone contemplating wealth preservation and international diversification must understand two U.S. government concepts: **income tax** and **reportable assets.**

If you hold assets offshore, some are reportable to the government and some are not. And if you make income while overseas, it is all reportable, although some of it is exempt (the first $97,600 a year, plus a $15,616 housing allowance).

In these tips, we've listed ways to legally avoid both reporting assets and paying income taxes while your assets are overseas.

The only drawback is CIBL charges monthly service fees for checking and savings (up to $12.50).

If you're interested in Caye Bank and need help setting things up, contact Kate Corrigan at: kcorrigan@cayebank.bz or go to the website at www.cayebank.bz. Just DON'T tell them I sent you! And for that matter, don't tell anyone else.

Alternately, if you want to avoid the big fees, you can look to open an account with a Canadian bank. Most charge a nominal fee or none at all. The drawback here is you'll have to physically visit Canada.

TIP No. 2: Buy a Little Bit of Land

Real estate is perhaps the best way of keeping assets overseas. The reason is simple. *It's not reportable.* And if it generates no income, you pay no tax on it either. Some of the smartest folks I know invested in foreign real estate and now have millions of dollars in assets offshore and out of reach of the government.

Also, several countries (Panama and Costa Rica, for example) allow you to invest in real estate and even sustainable timber farms. With enough money invested, you can get a permanent visa and even citizenship after five years with little or no questions asked. In addition, real estate can be made more liquid if you place it in a corporation or trust. This makes it easier to sell or transfer your assets.

The publications *International Living* and *Live and Invest Overseas* are two great resources for learning more about international real estate opportunities. You can learn more at their websites: www.internationalliving.com and www.liveandinvestoverseas.com.

TIP No. 3: Gold in the Bank

And last, my absolute favorite tip for keeping wealth out of the United States...

Bullion gold and silver (and other metals) are not reportable, nor do they generate taxable income until you sell them. So keeping bullion in a private and secure place outside the U.S. is a simple way to hold (and move) assets out of the country.

One of the simplest ways to do this is opening a safe deposit box in Canada. All you need to open a Canadian safe deposit box are two forms of identification – a passport and a driver's license will do – and an in-person visit to the bank. (This can vary slightly depending on the bank, so call the bank you're interested in first.)

One bank you can open a safe deposit box with is the Royal Bank of Canada (www.rbcroyalbank.com). Some banks do not allow you to store currency or legal tender in a safe deposit box. So call the bank you're interested before making the trip.

You can use your box to store precious metals, cash, and other items you want out of the U.S. government's eyes. And the box fees are similar to the fees you'd pay at an American bank.

Transporting your gold to Canada may seem frightening to some people. I've heard stories of people having their gold confiscated by ignorant customs officials. But taking gold into Canada is 100% legal as long as you declare it to customs. (You have to declare any amount of currency over $10,000.)

Of course, it's also risky to carry large amounts of gold as you travel. So...

If you don't want to handle transporting precious metals or cash to Canada yourself, you can use a professional transport service. Although this can be expensive if you're only moving a small amount of wealth.

A third option is to purchase your gold or silver in Canada. This means you don't have to carry large amounts of cash or precious metals while you travel.

PART FOUR

Secrets of the
Silver Market

— Chapter 1 —

Owning Silver Is the Best Decision You Can Make

Over the past few years, we've received hundreds and hundreds of angry letters, and many from people who say they never want to hear another word from us ever again... all because I've been describing the actions of the Obama administration as "The End of America."

I know, most Americans think I'm absolutely crazy. But I believe we are facing a major monetary crisis.

And the funny thing is... Everything I've said would happen is happening. Gold climbed from $700 in December 2008 to $1,200 per ounce in March 2015. Silver rose about 50%.

You simply can't create money at the rate we have and service this much debt over the long term.

That's the bad news.

The good news in all of this is we have an easy and predictable way to make a heck of a lot of money.

Yes, you should own some gold and silver... but I also believe you should know about one precious-metal stock that could prove incredibly lucrative over the next few years.

Before I give you all the details... let me back up a bit and explain why I think silver is such an important asset to own...

So why are we so bullish on silver? History.

No other investment asset loves a monetary crisis like silver does.

I would urge (even beg) you to read (and reread) the May 2006 issue of *Stansberry's Investment Advisory*. It explains in great detail the reasons why silver prices tend to soar during a monetary crisis. It also explains the three phases of a monetary crisis.

Back then, I explained why we were on the cusp of entering the second phase of a monetary crisis, which I defined this way...

> Phase II happens as the government begins to take actions to halt rising prices through force. The government will not cut its own spending, which is the primary driver of inflation... It will not begin to address the unsustainable nature of entitlement spending, or the current value of its long-tail obligations...
>
> Instead of addressing the genuine causes of inflation in the United States, the government will begin to tax, regulate, and even imprison what it labels the culprits. These efforts will only exacerbate and accelerate the rise in prices... Once Phase II begins, more and more people have tangible evidence that something has gone badly wrong with the economy. They begin to hoard. <u>Rich people hoard gold and silver.</u>

After I wrote those words, the annual government deficit soared from less than $300 billion to around $700 billion annually. The U.S. government continues to foster a soak-the-rich, tax-and-regulate regime, in which a dozen or more states have enacted steeply progressive "millionaire" taxes. Obama has personally lobbied the American people for more taxes on the "rich" – all of which have been used to justify more government spending and ever-larger government deficits.

Meanwhile, the inflation and the joblessness these policies cause have led to a return to "misery index"' conditions in the United States and more social unrest. I wish I could tell you the worst was over and our leaders will soon come to their senses and return our country to sound economic policies. But that will not happen.

Instead, the political dynamic in our country – where criminals run wild on the streets (and in the halls of Congress) while the government continues to print money to pay its debts – will lead to what I call a "Phase III" monetary crisis.

In a Phase III crisis, people flee from the currency at all costs. Civil society falls apart. Cash savings are destroyed and other forms of savings that depend on a stable currency – like insurance policies – are wiped out, too. Worst of all, the monetary crisis makes it impossible for people to save or invest in America. Our standard of living and our stature in the world collapse.

That's what's going to happen. I can't tell you exactly when. But the sure way to know how bad things are getting is to watch the Treasury markets...

As long as the world continues to buy our bonds, we're safe. But a moment will arrive – and it won't be long – when investors simply refuse to own our government's debt at almost any price. *If you don't take steps right now to protect yourself, you will be wiped out when that moment arrives.*

The best thing you can do about it is to own precious metals... especially silver. Owning silver and gold gives you real money that the politicians can't devalue and will have a hard time trying to confiscate – especially if you store it overseas. I recommend silver over gold.

And if you're going to buy silver, you must understand the silver ratio...

The market for silver has two distinct phases. First are the times when silver trades alongside gold as money.

During these periods, there's vast global demand for silver. When gold was the world's reserve currency and silver was also used as money, silver prices averaged around 1/16 the price of gold.

On the other hand, during periods where silver was "demonetized" – when it was not commonly used as money – this ratio to gold would become completely unpegged. In 1991, for example, an ounce of silver traded for only 1/100 the price of an ounce of gold.

When I first began to perceive we were in the early stages of a huge monetary crisis, I recommended readers add silver bullion to their portfolios as a hedge against the risk of hyperinflation. Back then, silver was trading at around $14. Gold was trading for around $675. Thus, the silver ratio stood at around 50. That is, silver was trading at 1/50 the price of gold.

In 2014, gold is trading for about $1,200. Silver is trading around $16. Investors who took my advice and began to stockpile precious metals have done very well.

But here's the really interesting part. In 2014, the silver ratio is around 75 – even higher than it was back in 2006. But the risks of a massive inflation have grown dramatically.

I believe silver is, by far, the better buy of the two precious metals.

Silver should be trading at a ratio of 20-25. That would put silver's price somewhere around $49 per ounce to $61 per ounce.

You have a lot of ways to invest in silver... But my colleague Dr. David Eifrig has researched an excellent way that allows individuals to take physical possession of silver without paying huge markups to the spot price (like you would buying rare coins). It doesn't require any risky leverage or buying of mining companies that may or may not be around this time next year.

Dr. Eifrig wrote about this unique opportunity to own real, hold-in-your-hand silver for less than $3 for his *Retirement Millionaire* subscribers... and he has agreed to let me share it with you as well...

A Silver Investment Created by the U.S. Government

By Dr. David Eifrig

The opportunity to own this type of silver began more than 200 years ago, when Congress designated silver as the material for the U.S.' first coin. Congress based its new dollar on the Spanish piaster, though it took its name from a German coin called the thaler.

Congress passed the U.S. Coinage Act of 1792, which laid out the specifications for all of its new coins. It set the standards we lay out below. (You'll notice the name for dimes is "dismes." That's not a typo – it's from the Latin decima.)

The highlighted coins marked below are those that we've found hold the best value.

However, based on our valuations as of late 2014, none are trading at a discount to their silver content. For now, we recommend waiting until you can buy these coins at a discount.

Eagles	$10	247 4/8 grain (16.0 g) pure or 270 grain (17.5 g) standard gold
Half Eagles	$5	123 6/8 grain (8.02 g) pure or 135 grain (8.75 g) standard gold
Quarter Eagles	$2.50	61 7/8 grain (4.01 g) pure or 67 4/8 grain (4.37 g) standard gold
Dollars or Units	$1	371 4/16 grain (24.1 g) pure or 416 grain (27.0 g) standard silver
Half Dollars	**$0.50**	**185 10/16 grain (12.0 g) pure or 208 grain (13.5 g) standard silver**
Quarter Dollars	**$0.25**	**92 13/16 grain (6.01 g) pure or 104 grains (6.74 g) standard silver**
Dismes	**$0.10**	**37 2/16 grain (2.41 g) pure or 41 3/5 grain (2.70 g) standard silver**
Half Dismes	**$0.05**	**18 9/16 grain (1.20 g) pure or 20 4/5 grain (1.35 g) standard silver**
Cents	$0.01	11 pennyweights (17.1 g) of copper
Half Cents	$0.005	5 1/2 pennyweights (8.55 g) of copper

* 28.34 grams = 1 ounce

That was the composition of U.S. coins for nearly 200 years, until the Coinage Act of 1965 **removed most of the silver from its coins.** Half dollars changed from 90% silver to 40% silver... And other coins were 75% copper and 25% nickel.

Then in 1970, Congress pulled the remaining silver from the coins.

Coins dated before 1965 are known as "junk silver." They get tagged as "junk" because they have no value to collectors. They circulated widely in pockets and purses and show a lot of wear. By one estimate, more than 13 billion of these coins are spread around the country.

But what's bad for collectors is great for us as investors.

Because they don't have collectible value, these coins can be purchased at just a few percentage points above the spot price for an ounce of silver.

That's significant since collectible and uncirculated silver coins often have premiums of 25%-50% or more than the spot price. So junk silver gives us an immediate 25%-30% discount to other types of silver coins.

How do you buy it? Junk silver comes in $1,000 face-value bags of either dimes, quarters, or half dollars. So the breakdown of a bag could be any of the following three:

• 10,000 dimes
• 4,000 quarters
• 2,000 half-dollar

Regardless of which denomination you choose, the amount of silver you are buying is the same... about 715-720 ounces.

The retail price for a $1,000 face-value bag of dimes, quarters, or half dollars in 2014 is about $16,800, plus shipping and insurance (which vary depending upon the delivery location, usually ranging from $60-$120).

So let's say the total cost is about $16,900. (By the way, many dealers will split bags into smaller bags to fit your budget... we'll give you the name of one in this chapter.)

Now, take $16,900 and divide it by 10,000 dimes and you get real, hold-in-your-hand silver for just $1.69. (Keep in mind, this value can fluctuate daily with the price of silver and with demand.) And that's why we say you can get silver for less than $3.

As the price and demand for silver increase, so will the value of your "junk silver."

But remember, silver is volatile. Any change in the price of silver could change your total cost. For the most current price, you can call either of the dealers I recommend in this chapter.

Plus, growing demand will push up dealer premiums on junk silver, further multiplying your gains.

In addition to the 25%-30% discount you get buying junk silver, you have four other reasons to own these coins rather than bullion, exchange-traded funds, mining stocks, or collectible coins:

90% of silver coins are well recognized – These coins are already well known. The fact is, you rarely find them in day-to-day circulation because people have already gone through their change looking for these valuable coins. And as precious-metal demand increases, even more people will recognize the coins.

90% of silver coins are easily divisible – Unlike a silver bar or gold coin, junk silver coins are already portioned in smaller amounts should you ever need to use it in everyday transactions.

90% of silver coins are liquid – There has always been a demand for these types of coins. Thanks to a dealer network and places like eBay, plenty of buyers are available should you ever want to cash in your gains.

90% of silver coins do not require verification – The silver content of these coins is so widely understood, you don't need to verify the authenticity and value. Again, there's no collectible value, and everyone understands they're 90% silver.

Chapter 3

Where to Get Your U.S. Coins

Buying silver and gold can be a risky business if you do not know who you are dealing with. Over the years, we at Stansberry Research have formed some reliable contacts in all areas of the financial world. Here are a few folks who "hoard" pre-1965 silver coins... and feel free to tell them we sent you. (Also, be sure to let me know your experience dealing with them.)

The names are:

Van Simmons
David Hall Rare Coins
P.O. Box 6220
Newport Beach, CA 92658
Phone: 800-759-7575 or 949-567-1325
E-mail: info@davidhall.com

Rich Checkan
Asset Strategies International
1700 Rockville Pike, Suite 400
Rockville, MD 20852
Phone: 800-831-0007 or 301-881-8600
Fax: 301-881-1936
E-mail: moreinfo@assetstrategies.com

Parker Vogt
Camino Coin 1301 Broadway Ave.
Burlingame, CA 94010
Phone: 800-348-8001 or 650-348-3000
E-mail: Parker@caminocompany.com

Rest assured, we receive no compensation for mentioning them.

Remember, you can always check the live price of silver at:
www.bulliondirect.com.

Chapter 4

Safe Silver: A Far Better Business

We think Dr. Eifrig's "junk silver" strategy is an excellent way to hold some physical gold and silver (particularly silver) to protect against a currency crisis.

But to capture greater gains as panicked investors rush to bullion, I like to own silver companies. Silver companies follow the movement of the underlying metal while also providing leverage. If we own silver bullion, we only make the price increase of silver. If we own a silver company, we can earn much, much more.

Silver Wheaton (NYSE: SLW) is the largest silver streamer in the world.

A "silver streamer" is essentially a company that purchases the silver byproduct from base-metal miners. Simply put, when a copper miner (or zinc miner or iron miner) extracts ore from his mine, that rock likely includes a lot of minerals other than copper – including silver. The copper miner doesn't want the hassle of smelting and dealing with the silver from his mine.

Approximately 70% of the world's silver is produced as a byproduct from other metal mines... So a silver streamer, like Silver Wheaton, is there to take it off his hands.

Silver Wheaton will swoop in and make a deal upfront for the silver. It's a good deal for the base-metal miner because he gets guaranteed income for his silver. And it's a great deal for Silver Wheaton because it gets a guaranteed supply of silver without the hassles and risks of actually mining it.

Silver Wheaton has dozens of long-term agreements across 23 gold and silver mining assets with companies like Barrick, Goldcorp, Glencore Mining, and Lundin Mining. In 2013, Silver Wheaton's streaming agreements produced about 26.8 million ounces of silver equivalent in 2013. Over time, other mines already covered by agreements with Silver Wheaton will be built, and the company expects production to hit 48 million silver ounces by 2018.

To understand exactly how these deals work, let's look at Silver Wheaton's agreement at Peñasquito, the second-largest mine in Mexico. It's a world-class gold/silver/lead/zinc deposit.

Silver Wheaton's flagship deal is an agreement with Goldcorp for 25% of the silver produced at the Peñasquito mine... for the life of the mine. This is the largest silver deposit in the world. Even a 25% stake ranks among the planet's top 20 silver deposits.

In April 2007, Silver Wheaton paid Goldcorp $485 million. At full capacity, the company expects to average 28 million ounces of silver per year for 13 years. That's an average of 7 million ounces per year for Silver Wheaton.

In 2013, the company sold 5,317 ounces of silver from Peñasquito for an average price of $23.81 per ounce. The average cash cost per ounce was a mere $4.12. That means the company's profit from each ounce of silver was $19.69.

Silver Wheaton's fundamentals are nearly perfect... This company has negligible debt, billions of ounces of silver equivalent reserves, an operating margin of around 50%, and a secure cash flow from mines in 10 countries. By 2017, it will produce about 53 million ounces of silver. That's almost double last year's production.

Silver Wheaton's strategy has paid off so far... but its results will get even better as the price of silver rises.

Silver Wheaton's costs are fixed. So as we saw with the Peñasquito example, any increase in the silver price goes straight to its net profit. According to the company's third-quarter 2014 filings, it pays an average of $4.16 per ounce of silver it receives. If you look at Silver Wheaton's share price compared with its earnings, you'll see a direct relationship to the price of silver. In other words, as the silver price goes up, people will pay more for the stock.

That means a rise in the silver price gives your investment "juice."

Of course, the leverage works both ways. When the metal sells off, so do the shares in Silver Wheaton.

When investing in trophy-asset companies like Silver Wheaton, we like to compare the company's market cap with the value of its tangible assets. Our aim is to buy a company when its market cap trades at a discount to its tangible assets. At least 25%... higher if possible.

We've analyzed Silver Wheaton's numbers going back to 2005. It turns out, the last time we could buy the company at a discount to total assets was back in October and November 2008. During that time, you could have bought the company for up to a 30% discount to total assets. The stock soared from lows around $3 per share at that time to as high as $47 in early 2011 when silver was also trading at multiyear highs of about $48 per ounce.

As of September 30, 2014, the company's total assets equal $4.3 billion. The company carries no goodwill or intangible assets on its balance sheet, so we'll use its total assets valuation. At the time of writing this, the company's market cap sits around $7.7 billion. That's a 79% premium based on its total assets valuation.

But remember this: **From 2004 to 2014, total assets have grown from $156 million to $4.3 billion**. That's massive growth in 10 years. Now, we don't expect growth to continue at such high rates. But looking at the past five years of data, the company still enjoyed an impressive 14% annual growth rate.

Given the recent selloff in the precious metals market, along with the company's ability to grow assets, we believe we'll get another opportunity to buy at a discount.

PART FIVE

Goldscam: How to Protect Yourself and Grow Rich

— Chapter 1 —

What Happens When They Won't Take Dollars Anymore?

If you've invested in gold, I urge you to think carefully about what you own – or *think* you own.

Demand for gold investments skyrocketed from 2003 to 2013 as the price of gold escalated from a little more than $250 an ounce in 2001 to its peak near $1,900 an ounce in 2011...

Some people invested in the precious metal as a way to protect themselves against inflation and a weakening dollar. Others simply wanted to jump onboard a historic bull market. Whatever their reasons... more and more investors are seeking precious-metal investments. It has created virtually unprecedented demand for gold (and silver) investments.

These folks have the right idea... We've advocated gold ownership for years.

The problem is, owning gold – truly having physical possession of some amount of the metal – can be inconvenient. It requires some effort and planning to transport and store, especially if you want to hold a lot of it.

So the financial industry has responded as it always does... selling folks the investments they want.

In this case, the financial industry has created convenient ways for people to put their money in the gold market. These investments can take different forms, but essentially people invest their money and receive a certificate or document that they understand to represent a claim on some amount of gold.

These instruments are liquid and easy to buy and sell. That makes them appealing to nonprofessionals, which is the whole point. And lots of people have invested in gold through a variety of these financial vehicles.

Unfortunately, many of these people assume this gold is being stored in a safe place, guarded and accounted for, available when they need it. My guess is, many of these people have a terrible surprise awaiting them.

These investment vehicles represent a volume of gold that simply doesn't exist in the world. It's a phenomenon we've labeled "Goldscam." **The only way to ensure your gold investments are completely safe is to avoid any sort of paper claim on gold... and have real, physical gold in your possession**.

At the heart of Goldscam is this simple fact...

According to U.S. Geological Survey records, for every 400 ounces of gold that are traded via "futures" contracts on the American commodities exchange (known as COMEX), only one ounce actually exists in the exchange's vaults. That's around $1,600 worth of assets covering $640,000 worth of trades.

On a typical trading day, contracts representing as many as 18 million ounces of gold can trade hands. Most people are simply betting on which way the price will go, without ever intending to take delivery. They settle their contracts with dollars.

Now, it's not unusual for commodity markets to operate this way. Futures contracts of every kind trade in multiples. And today, the options market runs smoothly because many people are still willing to trade their gold for dollars.

But I believe that at some point they won't...

I believe we're approaching a day when people will no longer exchange their dollars for gold.

As you know, our country is in a precarious financial position. I'm sure you've heard the countless stories about the enormity of our national debt. I've written volumes about it myself.

The numbers are too large to truly comprehend. We've borrowed so many trillions of dollars, it's impossible for us to pay back any of this money by honest means. Our only option is to print an endless stream of dollars to meet those obligations...

And that's what our government is doing. The Federal Reserve calls it "quantitative easing." It's simply the process of creating more dollars.

However, the more we print, the less each dollar is worth. Eventually, our creditors will no longer accept the dollar. When the global financial industry loses faith completely in the U.S. dollar, it will look for another sound currency. It will want gold...

And once we reach that tipping point... those who hold futures contracts that give them the right to receive gold will demand delivery. They won't take dollars in exchange.

But remember... it's impossible that all the gold that people supposedly have the "right" to actually exists. I can't say exactly what will happen to gold exchange-traded funds during that kind of run on the gold futures market... But I believe any investment vehicle based on these futures will be in trouble.

I realize I'm describing an extreme situation. And so long as people are content to hold paper claims on gold, no problem... But what happens when people realize their paper claims are worthless and want to take possession of the actual bullion?

Many people, myself included, have lost complete faith in the U.S. dollar.

I'll never sell a single ounce of my gold for U.S. dollars – not at any price. And I'm putting as much of my money as possible into other hard assets, like real estate.

I firmly believe this will soon become the mainstream opinion. And many of the folks who have bought gold investments will discover what they really own is paper as worthless as the dollar.

On the other hand, the value of actual, real, hold-in-your-hand gold will explode...

Now, to be clear, when we call this phenomenon "Goldscam," I'm not accusing anyone of a specific crime. The futures market operates as it was designed to do. And the financial services industry is offering legal products based off that market.

What I'm referring to is the belief investors have been encouraged to hold... that their gold investments are as good as holding real, physical gold. It's not. In a true crisis, there's no substitute for having a store of precious metals in your possession.

That's why I urge everyone to own real, physical, hold-in-your-hand gold. In a true run on gold, the value of the actual physical asset will soar to outrageous levels...

There are a number of ways to acquire physical gold. For the typical American, the best place to start is with the **modern bullion coins** we talked about in Part Four. The most widely traded gold coin is the U.S. Gold Eagle. If you're new to gold, the U.S. Gold Eagles are the way to go.

You can buy them from most dealers. They're easy to store and can be shipped safely by registered mail or Federal Express.

Some gold buyers also like to own South African Krugerrands or Canadian Maple Leafs. Those are fine bullion coins. But bear in mind, when you buy those foreign coins, the dealer must fill out a 1099 form with the IRS. When you buy Gold Eagles, it does not need to be reported to the IRS.

However, there's an even better way to own physical gold: **Rare gold (and silver) coins**. In this section, I'll show you why. I'll also describe – with the help of one of the world's foremost experts on gold and silver coins – how to buy them and what price you can expect to pay.

But first, let me show you some of the benefits of adding rare coins to your investment portfolio...

Chapter 2

The Benefits of Buying Rare Coins

Rare gold and silver coins are a fantastic form of concentrated wealth. You can put five or 10 coins in a briefcase and literally take hundreds of thousands, even millions, of dollars anywhere in the world.

In the U.S., the rare coin market is about $5 billion a year (and that excludes all the bullion coins sold and all the coin items the U.S. Mint sells to collectors).

Europe has a huge market for rare coins from around the world, including U.S. coins. Europe *exports* approximately $300 million worth of our gold coins back to the U.S. each year. And European coin auctions regularly feature U.S. coins.

Asia, Tokyo, and Hong Kong have had an active market for decades. Markets are rapidly opening up in mainland China, and demand is huge.

When it comes to the best ways to buy rare coins, I turn to Van Simmons and David Hall. They are, hands down, the smartest gold and silver coin investors I've ever met.

Van and David have been buying and selling gold and silver coins

The Smartest Gold and Silver Coin Investors I've Ever Met

In 1986, Van and David co-founded a business called PCGS... or the Professional Coin Grading Service. This service revolutionized the coin industry. It made coin prices transparent.

They hired rare-coin experts and asked them to grade billions of dollars' of coins. After grading the coins, the experts sealed them in airtight plastic wallets.

The plastic wallet acted like a guarantee of authenticity. Novice investors could trade coins with other novice investors without knowing anything about coin grading.

PCGS became a successful business. It's the top grading service in the world.

(and rare coins) for more than 40 years. They know how the markets work and the best coins to buy.

Here are Van's reasons for adding rare coins to an investment portfolio...

First, **these coins represent an "island of safety" from currency fluctuations**. Their intrinsic value and desirability are not dependent on what's going on with the dollar, the euro, or any other individual currencies.

They're also saleable in almost any place on Earth in a wide range of currencies, as opposed to many traditional assets that are denominated in dollars.

A second benefit is **anonymity**. Rare coins are a way to hold some of your wealth without showing up on *Forbes'* list of the wealthiest Americans. Things like real estate, stocks, and bonds can be easily tracked. On the other hand, owning rare coins is a way of taking your wealth out of view of almost anyone who wants to know what you own.

Third, **unlike most other investments, rare coins are things that you can actually enjoy**. David says that rare coins are literally "history in your hands." You can buy a rare coin, hold it in your hand, and enjoy the history of it.

Finally, **rare coins are an anti-confiscation hedge**. The last time gold ownership was illegal in the United States (1933-1975), holding rare gold and silver coins was not illegal. Even President Roosevelt, with all his power at the height of the Depression, did not make rare coin ownership illegal.

Five Key Considerations

There are five key ideas that apply to investing in rare coins. As Van explains...

First, and probably most important, you need to find a dealer who's honest and is going to treat you fairly.

One thing to look for is a dealer who offers a buy/sell spread and will guarantee to buy rare coins back... In this business, reputable dealers will agree to buy their coins back and tell you exactly what they'll pay for it.

Of course, many dealers will say, "Gee, I'm sorry, we don't buy stuff back." What that usually means is they overcharged you so badly to begin with, they don't want to tell you what they're actually willing to pay you now...

Finding a reputable dealer largely depends on the market. You can start by talking with and asking questions to a lot of dealers...

You can join clubs and attend events. When you talk to members, inevitably there'll be one or two names that pop up as the most popular dealers.

There are also a million books and websites dedicated to rare coins now that can give you a better understanding of that particular market and help you find a dealer you can trust.

If you do your homework – and if you learn what is important and what isn't, or what has value and what doesn't – it makes it hard for a dealer and other rare coin collectors to take advantage of you...

In general, it's almost always better to try and work with a dealer who owns a business as opposed to a salesman. If you deal with the people who own the business, you're dealing with somebody who has a reputation at stake.

There's a reason that Van has kept clients for 25 or 30 years... It's because as a business owner, you try to do the best job you can do. If you're dealing with one of the principals of the business, it usually limits your risk. More often than not, they're going to do what's in the client's best interest because that's in their long-term best interest, also.

The second key, according to Van, is generally to avoid buying any coins that are relatively new, like one that may have just been struck from the Franklin Mint...

It usually takes 40 or 50 years for something to become "rare"... a true collectible. So it's a gamble to buy something today hoping in 40 or 50 years it's going to become desirable. There's simply no way to know what's going to be popular 50 years from now.

You're much better off buying a rare coin that has a long track record... that has already been a popular collectible for many decades and has a large, well-established collector base. The more popular and the bigger the collector base, generally the more liquid the market for that coin is and the better the price will be when you decide you would like to sell.

The third key is to buy rare coins when prices may not have seen much movement for a period of time, or if the market corrects significantly and leaves prices too low...

Like in other markets, these are the times when you're most likely to find rare coins trading at great values. Of course, the hardest thing to do is buy in a bear market. It's not easy to be a contrarian and buy when things are cheap and undervalued... but that's one of the keys to big returns. When you buy a great asset at a great value, your chances of success go up exponentially.

The fourth key – and this is a bit different than some other investments – is to "buy what you like"...

If you buy a coin because it's beautiful, in great condition, and you really like it, chances are somebody else will like it for similar reasons. So there's an added dimension you don't find in many other assets.

The fifth and final key is the biggest consideration for investors in the rare coin market: condition and grading. You want to buy coins that are graded by a third-party grading service...

Van only sells PCGS [Professional Coin Grading Service] coins. Granted, he's biased because he helped found the company. But the point is, in most cases, PCGS coins sell for the most money. There's a reason a coin graded by PCGS will sell for $20,000 and a similar coin graded by another company will sell for $10,000 to $15,000 in the same grade.

So you have to buy something that's authentic and correctly evaluated and graded. In the coin market, you don't want to end up with something that's been doctored, tooled, re-toned, or anything else. You want a coin that some third-party authentication group has looked at, verified as being in the correct condition, and will stand behind it with a money-back guarantee.

Generally speaking, the better the condition and the rarer the coin, the more the coin will be worth. In most cases, it's best to stay with higher-quality items. If you aren't able to afford a particular high-quality rare coin, it's usually better to consider a different coin than to buy one of lower-quality.

Of course, the most rare items often can't be found in a high grades, and "ultra-rarities" are almost always desirable, regardless of condition. For example, a 1795 $5 Small Eagle – the first U.S. gold coin ever made – is very desirable and highly valued in any grade.

These are the big ideas that you should focus on if you're interested in rare coins.

People have been buying and selling coins for more than 2,000 years. (Wealthy Romans collected Greek coins.) And the U.S. has had an active coin market since the Civil War.

But we're not talking about collecting coins. We're concerned with financial survival. We're concerned with protecting – and growing – our net worth from the inevitable decline in the value of the U.S. dollar. With that in mind, let's talk about the best gold and silver coins for "financial survival."

I asked Van and David to recommend the ultimate "financial survival guide" for buying gold and silver coins. They wrote about every type of coin, from straight gold and silver bullion to ultra-rarities.

In the next chapter, they discuss how to navigate the rare coin market. This unique type of hold-in-your-hand gold and silver bullion has NEVER been confiscated by the government. And buying them is one of the best ways to ensure your financial survival during the continued decline of the U.S. dollar.

— Chapter 3 —

Vintage Gold and Silver Bullion Coins

By Van Simmons and David Hall, Professional Coin Grading Service

There are vintage U.S. gold coins (pre-1933) and silver coins (pre-1965) that sell for a small premium over their bullion value.

They are an excellent way to hold gold and silver as financial survival coins. They are also an anti-confiscation hedge. We (Van and David) think it's unlikely that gold ownership will be made illegal in this country, but there is some chance it could happen.

The last time gold ownership was illegal in the United States (1933-1975), holding vintage gold and silver coins was not illegal. Even FDR, with all his power at the height of the Depression, did not make vintage coin ownership illegal.

The vintage gold and silver coins that sell for very small premiums over their bullion content are as follows:

$20 Liberties circa 1880-1907 (in circulated condition)

These coins have 0.9765 ounces of gold. They are the largest regular issue United States gold coins and were one of the bullion coins of choice for international trade and transactions (along with the English Sovereign, French 20 Franc, and Swiss 20 Franc) from roughly 1880 to about 1970 or so.

These coins trade in the grades of Very Fine (VF) to Extremely Fine (XF) and have just a little bit of wear. They currently sell for somewhere around 20% over their bullion content. But you aren't really overpaying for bullion since when it's time to sell, they bring considerably more than their bullion price.

Historically, the premium on these coins has gotten as high as 100% over the price of bullion.

$20 St. Gaudens circa 1908-1928 (in uncirculated condition)

The $20 St. Gaudens is one of the world's most famous coins. It didn't see a lot of circulation at the time of issue, as it was used mostly for international trade and interbank payments. Consequently, most survivors are in lower-grade uncirculated condition (known as "Commercial Uncs" in the trade).

Like the circulated $20 Liberties, they are currently selling for 12%-18% or so over their bullion content and are great financial survival coins.

Pre-1965 U.S. 90% silver coins

Between 1794 and 1964, U.S. dimes, quarters, and half dollars were 90% silver. But in the early 1960s, years of government deficit spending and inflation had eroded the value of the U.S. dollar to such an extent that the silver in the coins was worth more than the face value of the coins.

It was nothing like the deficit spending and inflation we've been subject to since, but it was definitely a minor preview of things to come. In 1965, the 90% silver coins were replaced by the copper-nickel coins we have today. The 90% pre-1965 silver coins have traded for a premium over face value... a gradually increasing premium... since 1965.

In modern times, pre-1965 90% silver coins sell for 10%-15% over their silver melt value. It doesn't matter whether they are dimes, quarters, or half dollars. As long as they are pre-1965, there is a big liquid market and they work great as financial survival coins.

1878-1935 silver dollars

Silver dollars were minted in the U.S. between 1794 and 1935. The 1878-1921 Morgan dollars and 1921-1935 Peace dollars were minted by the hundreds of millions. Millions of them survive today.

Like the 90% silver dimes, quarters, and half dollars, circulated examples of the 90% silver 1878-1935 dollars trade for 10%-15% of their silver melt value. These coins basically trade in three groups: the 1878-1904 Morgan dollars, the 1921 Morgan dollar, and the 1922-1935 Peace dollars. (The 1921 Peace dollar is a rare date.)

We like 1922-1935 Peace dollars, in particular. Collectors flock to the "old stuff," like the 1878-1904 Morgans. But for someone who wants the metal, the Peace Dollars are a better value.

Semi-Numismatic Gold Coins

There is a large market for higher-grade, vintage U.S. gold coins, the so-called semi-numismatic gold coins.

The most heavily traded semi-numismatic gold coins are the $20 St. Gaudens (circa 1908-1928) and the $20 Liberty (circa 1900-1907). The semi-numismatic grades traded most frequently are MS62 to MS65. That's Average Uncirculated MS62, Choice Uncirculated MS63, Near Gem Uncirculated MS64, and Gem Uncirculated MS65. As you might expect, the lower the grade, the lower the premium over the gold-melt value.

We like the MS63 $20 St. Gaudens. For semi-numismatic gold, it's all about the premium. And the premium can fluctuate... a lot. Smart gold coin buyers watch the premiums closely. A few of the largest gold coin wholesalers play the premium with coin shorts and gold hedges.

When premiums are low for a certain grade, they will load up on the coins and short gold on the commodity exchanges. When premiums are high, they will short the coins (by advance selling to retailers for future delivery) and go long gold on the commodity exchanges. In terms of their actual gold position, they are flat... But they are speculating on the rise or fall of the coin premiums.

We like MS63 $20 St. Gaudens because premiums are historically low. Premiums often decrease when gold bullion prices run up sharply, as it usually takes a while for the coins to "catch up." MS63 $20 St. Gaudens (PCGS-graded for highest quality assurance and most resale value) are between 20% and 30%. Over the past 25 years, the premium has usually fluctuated between 50% and 125%.

While the low premium lasts, we like the PCGS-graded MS63 $20 St. Gaudens best out of all the semi-numismatic gold coins. Note that you can also buy the $2.50, $5, and $10 pre-1933 semi-numismatic gold coins.

Classic Gold and Silver Coin Rarities

What are the rare U.S. coins that are high-demand, liquid items world-wide? Which U.S. coins can you put in a briefcase and take to Paris, Hong Kong, New York, or even L.A., for that matter?

The right coins for concentrated wealth survival and transfer are the classic gold and silver rarities, the high demand, well-known, long-term rarities of the U.S. coin market.

We have identified 22 gold coins (and coin types) and 18 silver coins that are the cream of the classic coin rarity crop. You can get a copy of the list of all 40 coins by request from our office, or you can call us and we'll talk about them with you.

These classic gold and silver rarities sell for as little as $2,000-$4,000 per coin and as much as $300,000-$400,000 per coin. Most of them are in the $10,000-$100,000 per coin price range.

Here are two examples of fantastic, high-demand, classic rarities. The 1795 $5 and 1795 $10 gold pieces were the first gold coins struck by the new United States. For the 1795 $10, a mere 5,583 coins were originally minted. Of those, probably 300-500 survive today.

Also note that in 1834, the gold content of U.S. coins was lowered slightly (our first devaluation and a preview of things to come). So most of the pre-1834 gold coins hit the melting pot.

In modern times, the 1795 $10 gold piece is a super-high-demand, incredibly well-known coin worldwide. An almost uncirculated example (say a PCGS-graded AU55) goes for about $75,000.

For a classic silver rarity, check out the 1836 Gobrecht silver dollar. Silver dollars were struck between 1794 and 1803, but weren't struck between 1804 and 1835. The 1836 Gobrecht design silver dollar was the first silver dollar struck in 33 years and only 1600 were originally made. They sell for about $75,000 in the high grade of PR64.

Below is a price history of these two great coins. Please note... the price histories of the other classic gold and silver coin rarities are similar.

1795 $10 AU55

Year	Price
1970	$2,200
1990	$17,500
2000	$26,000
2011	$75,000

1836 Gobrecht silver dollar, PR64

Year	Price
1970	$1,900
1990	$35,000
2000	$37,500
2011	$75,000

Ultra Rarities

If your net worth is extremely large, U.S. coin ultra-rarities are a fantastic way to have a portion of your assets diversified into concentrated wealth survival and transfer coins.

The concept is the same as discussed previously with "Classic Gold and Silver Coin Rarities," except the ultra-rarities are million-dollar coins, and one of them is a nickel coin. There are about 20 ultra-rarities you could buy, stick in a briefcase, and go anywhere in the U.S., Europe, or Asia with an extremely saleable multimillion-dollar asset.

A perfect example of a gold, million-dollar coin ultra-rarity is the 1907 Extremely High Relief $20 St. Gaudens. This coin was designed by the world-renown sculptor Augustus St. Gaudens at the personal request of President Theodore Roosevelt. And it is one of the most beautiful coins ever made.

A mere 22 coins were made, and about 18-20 survive. They were all saved with special care, and survivors grade very high.

At a January 2007 auction, a PCGS-graded PR68 was bought at $1,840,000. Let's use that figure to examine the price history.

1907 Extremely High Relief $20 St. Gaudens, PR68

Year	Price
1970	$60,000
1990	$425,000
2000	$1,100,000
2007	$1,840,000

Please note... all U.S. coin ultra-rarities have the same spectacular price histories. And they don't even have to be gold or silver...

The most famous U.S. coin is the 1913 Liberty nickel. There were only five made. Today, two are in museums and three are privately held.

Here are some actual historical sales for this world-famous coin rarity. The 1913 Liberty nickel was the first coin to sell for $100,000 and also the first coin to sell for $1 million.

Year	Price
1941	$500 (private sale)
1943	$1,000 (private sale)
1954	$3,750 (auction)
1967	$46,000 (auction)
1972	$100,000 (private sale)
1985	$385,000 (auction)
1993	$962,500 (auction)
1996	$1,485,000 (auction)
2001	$1,840,000 (auction)
2010	$3,737,500 (auction)

Owners of 1913 Liberty nickels have included L.A. Lakers owner Dr. Jerry Buss and King Farouk of Egypt. So when we say "world-renown" when talking about ultra-rarities, we really mean "world-renown."

You obviously have to be very wealthy to participate in the ultra-rarity market, but these world-renown coins are definitely a great long-term store of value.

Start Building Your Financial Survival Gold and Silver Portfolio Immediately

Porter here again...

What are the right gold and silver coins for you to buy? It all depends on your personal situation, the amount of money you want to spend on gold and silver, and your comfort level with the various types of coins.

Those are personal decisions for you to make. No matter what size your portfolio is, it's never too late to begin building a financial survival stash of gold and silver coins.

To get the latest quotes – and the latest expert advice on where to find the greatest values in gold and silver coins – contact Van and David. You can reach them directly by phone (800-759-7575 or 949-567-1325) or through e-mail (info@davidhall.com).

I receive no compensation for recommending Van and David's services. I'm honored to introduce you to them. They are legends of the gold and silver business. And they have a long record of serving Stansberry Research subscribers with the best coin services you can find anywhere.

Chapter 4

How to Legally Smuggle Gold

By Dr. Steve Sjuggerud, editor, *True Wealth*

Porter note: There are two more strategies for holding physical gold that I want you to understand. The first is a simple way to keep your gold holdings with you... and even move them across national borders without drawing attention to yourself.

This following essay on how to legally "smuggle" gold was written by my longtime friend and colleague, Dr. Steve Sjuggerud...

———————————●———————————

Did you know the president confiscated all the gold of American citizens in 1933?

It's true... all in one quick swoop of the pen:

> UNDER THE EXECUTIVE ORDER OF THE PRESIDENT
>
> Issued April 5, 1933
>
> All persons are required to deliver ON OR BEFORE MAY 1, 1933 all GOLD COINS, GOLD BULLION, AND GOLD CERTIFICATES now owned by them to a Federal Reserve Bank, branch, or agency, or to any member bank of the Federal Reserve System.

It was the height of the Great Depression. And the U.S. government desperately needed to shore up its financial position. So in a dramatic move, it took everyone's gold.

Could it happen again? Well, put it this way: Who could have imagined it would happen the first time around?

Every day on the radio, I (Steve) hear ads about buying gold as a store of wealth. But folks who held gold as a store of wealth in the Great Depression had that "wealth" confiscated by the government.

My longtime friend Michael Checkan runs a business called Asset Strategies International. He finds legal ways to protect and diversify your wealth.

At lunch one day, Michael told me about a neat little idea he came up with. I thought the idea was worth sharing with you...

"When the U.S. government confiscated gold back in 1933," Michael told me, "you were allowed to keep your gold jewelry. The president didn't ask for Grandma's wedding ring."

For example, if you wanted to, you could carry 100 24-karat gold necklaces – each piece weighing one to five ounces – out of the country, and you wouldn't run afoul of the currency laws. And then you could convert them to money at most gold dealers in the world. It's like legal gold smuggling.

I don't recommend doing this on any scale. First off, you'd look like Mr. T. going through customs. And second, it's just not cost-effective... Most 24-karat jewelry is handmade and costs a premium over the price of gold. But a gold dealer will only pay you a discount to the gold price.

Finally, I'm not a lawyer, but I'm sure that if you tried to bring a load of high-end jewelry across the border, someone would decide you're somehow breaking a law.

However, for a small portion of your gold, jewelry is an interesting idea...

My friend and publisher of *The Palm Beach Letter* Tom Dyson was also at the lunch, and he was considering buying jewelry for his wife for this same reason. "My wife would like some jewelry... If I bought this, my wife would get something she wants to wear... and I'll be confident that it's not worthless. It has real gold value."

With this idea, you can keep your significant other happy while you're confident you own something with real value. And in the extreme case, if we see another 1933, your gold should be safe.

It's an interesting idea. For a small portion of your gold holdings, jewelry is worth considering...

To learn more about jewelry and other asset-diversification strategies, we recommend you talk to Michael. He is extremely knowledgeable and has offered to answer any questions for Stansberry Research readers. Visit his website at www.assetstrategies.com or call (800) 831-0007.

Chapter 5

How to Buy Bullion with No Markup

This finally strategy I want to share isn't for everyone... You have to be in a position to order a large amount of gold. But if you can make a large transaction quickly, it may be the best way to get an excellent price on bullion.

In this chapter, we describe how to buy physical gold off the Commodity Exchange (COMEX)... COMEX is ground-zero for the coming run on gold. So why would I suggest putting money in gold futures?

The key is to do this quickly... Use only the shortest-dated contracts to ensure you get delivery immediately before the crisis, while everything is operating normally. Once the run begins... this strategy will disappear...

The New York Mercantile Exchange (NYMEX) is the world's largest physical commodity futures exchange.

The futures exchange is a market like any other, where sellers and buyers agree on a price. The only difference, really, is that they don't settle up right away. They "lock in" the price for a future date.

COMEX is one of the two principal divisions of the NYMEX.

When you buy a gold futures contract on the COMEX, you agree to buy gold at a particular price on a particular date. Unfortunately, you can't buy just a few ounces of gold on the COMEX. Each gold contract covers 100 ounces of gold, in a 100-ounce "good delivery" bar.

So if you don't have the capital to cover 100 ounces of gold, try a couple of the other sources of cheap gold listed in this book. If you do have the capital, here's how it works...

Little gold actually changes hands on the COMEX. Most buyers and sellers of gold futures contracts are speculating on changes in the price of gold.

But every participant who buys a gold futures contract can request actual delivery of the gold.

To buy physical gold on the COMEX, you need to open an account with a futures broker. You can do this through a U.S. Futures Commission Merchant, like www.rjofutures.com. These brokers may ask you to prove a minimum net worth and a minimum income. If you can put down enough cash for 100 ounces of gold, you should clear these requirements no problem.

The most active months for trading gold futures contracts are February, April, June, August, October, and December. In other words, you have lots of choices for when to get your gold.

But if you want to get your gold as soon as possible, buy a futures contract for the current month. That contract will close ("settle") on the third-to-last business day of the month. Buy your contract and deposit the full amount into your account. In less than a month, you'll be the proud owner of 100 ounces of gold.

Now, you don't have to deposit the whole amount right away. You'll probably have to put down something like 10%. But if gold declines in price, you'll be required to deposit more or risk getting kicked out of the contract at a loss.

On the settlement date, your account will be charged for an amount equal to the settlement price (whatever the contract price was when you bought it) multiplied by the exact weight of the particular bar that's been assigned to you. (Bars can vary from 95 to 105 ounces.)

You won't pay any markup on the gold, but you will pay a commission ranging between $30 and $80. (These rates are paid per contract, so that's not even one-tenth of one percent.)

When you buy gold off the COMEX, it is stored in one of the four designated COMEX depositories, all of which are in or near New York City. The average storage fee is $15 a month per bar.

Ask your broker to mail you the warehouse receipt, which includes all the details on your specific bar. Don't lose this receipt.

You can get your bar delivered to your home, but you have to pay a $150 delivery fee to get the bar released. Then you'll have to add shipping charges on top of that.

If you leave your bar in the COMEX vaults, you know it's safe. And it's easier to sell this way. (A prospective buyer will not question the authenticity of your gold if it has been locked away in a monitored facility since you bought it.)

PART SIX

The World's Most Valuable Asset in a Time of Crisis

How You Can Protect Yourself – and Even Profit – in the Face of a Crisis

If things get as bad as I expect in America in the coming years, most people are going to lose a lot of money.

So how can you protect yourself... and even potentially make a profit over the next decade?

Well, you should own a significant amount of precious metals... real, hold-in-your-hand gold and silver. Both of these metals have skyrocketed between 1992 and 2012: Gold rose more than 450%, and silver increased nearly 800%. Both have pulled back more recently, but are still up over the long term.

But guess what...

There's one investment that might prove to be even better than gold or silver when America's currency crisis hits full tilt.

Since 1992, this investment has easily outpaced both stocks and gold, appreciating by more than 1,000%. And if you go back to 1971, a year before the U.S. went completely off the gold standard, the gains are even greater.

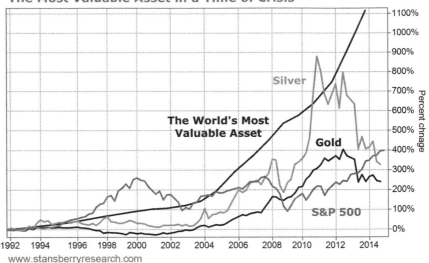

The Most Valuable Asset in a Time of Crisis

So what is this incredible asset that has crushed stocks and gold, and how does it beat these things handily?

We're talking about **farmland**. The chart above shows the total returns of U.S. farmland versus the total returns of gold and silver.

The returns from farmland come from the National Council of Real Estate Investment Fiduciaries. According to *Ag Decision Maker*, published by Iowa State University, roughly half of the overall returns come from the appreciation of the actual land.

The other half comes from the "rent" you can get by farming your land – or hiring someone else to do it for you. Add these components together, and it's easy to see why the overall returns of farmland have outpaced gold, stocks, and just about any other asset we could name.

Some call farmland "gold with yield" – because you book steady income from rents while you wait for the value to grow. I can think of no better asset to own during any kind of financial crisis.

Why does farmland do so well?

When food prices go up, farmland prices go up. There's no shortage of mouths to feed – on this side of the globe or the other.

And as an added benefit, farmland returns have little correlation to the returns on stocks and bonds. Farmland didn't fall in a single quarter during the financial meltdown.

If you believe, as I do, that inflation will only get worse, then you'll want to look closely at an investment in farmland.

Consider...

If you had invested your money in the stock market at the beginning of the 1970s, you would have made about 16%... TOTAL... over the course of the entire decade. Adjusted for inflation, you would have lost about half your money.

But during the same time, the total returns of U.S. farmland were more than 600%. Now imagine what farmland might do...

I can guarantee we are going to experience major inflation.

On top of that, other factors are pushing farmland prices higher...

Just to name a few: A tightening supply of farmland and rising demand for crops. In short, I expect farmland could be one of the best investments of the next decade.

Of course, farmland has another great benefit as well...

It can actually save your family during a serious crisis.

Barton Biggs, in his excellent book, *Wealth, War, and Wisdom,* reports farmland was the one thing that saved families in occupied France, Poland, Holland, Germany, and Italy.

> An unostentatious farm, not a great estate, is probably best. Bricks and mortar real estate can be expropriated or bombed, but the land is always there. Your land can't be plundered or shipped off to somewhere else.

> During World War II in most of the occupied countries, if you had a self-sufficient farm, you could hunker down on it and with luck wait out the disaster. At the very least you were supplied with food in a starving country.
>
> A working farm protected both your wealth and your life.

As my good friend (and multimillionaire investor) Doug Casey likes to say, in a time of crisis, "The best thing you can do is buy a really good farm."

We began writing about farmland as a "crisis asset" in 2010. Since then, market prices have confirmed our thesis. Iowa State University's annual survey of land values reports Iowa land prices increased 32.5% in 2011... followed by another 23.7% in 2012... and hit historic peaks in 2013.

Most people don't realize how important the black earth of Iowa and its neighboring states was to the formation of the American Empire. It's impossible to overstate it. To this day, the farmland of Middle America is a key component of America's geopolitical dominance.

This giant chunk of land is crisscrossed by an extensive network of navigable waterways. This allows America to produce stupendous amounts of food... and to efficiently transport that food (via ships) to markets.

There is simply no other region on Earth that can produce such huge amounts of food and ship it at such low cost. Farming this region allowed America to develop a massive, well-fed population. It allowed capital to flow into railroads, factories, and cities. It allowed the build-out of the most powerful military on Earth.

So what's the best way to capitalize on the booming farmland trend?

Well, just like I prefer owning real, hold-in-your-hand gold and silver rather than owning precious metals on the stock market... I suggest you **seriously consider a private land deal**. You should investigate buying a plot of farmland.

But if your only option is the stock market, there is one company that you should consider...

— Chapter 2 —

One of the Best 'Crisis Asset' Companies in the World

My favorite agricultural company is called **Cresud (Nasdaq: CRESY)**.

Cresud is run by one of the world's best investors, a man I'm almost sure you've never heard of, named Eduardo Elsztain.

I've been a longtime admirer of Eduardo, and I've gotten to know him on a personal level, too. He even invited me to ring the opening bell with him on the New York Stock Exchange in 2013 to commemorate a new business deal.

One of the things I love about Eduardo is he has survived and prospered through more government-debt pileups and busts than any big investor I'm aware of. You see, Eduardo has lived his life in Argentina, which has a history of wiping out investors time and again.

Eduardo's first-hand knowledge of how to invest through an inflationary time is important... as our U.S. government is inflating our money at an unprecedented, off-the-charts rate. To me, nobody is more experienced than Eduardo at profiting from this situation.

Cresud is Argentina's largest cattle raiser and owner of private farmland, with some of the world's best agricultural lands. The company's 600,000-acre Los Pozos farm is recorded on the books at its historic cost of around $4.50 an acre (plus improvements). That's the way accounting works. But according to a sale a few years ago, the land is worth as much as 25 times more than what is on the books.

The company is also the biggest owner of commercial real estate in one of the world's finest cities – Buenos Aires. Eduardo buys real estate (buildings) through a company he built called IRSA. He tries to buy it extremely cheaply, improve its value, and then sell it.

He does this because real property is a proven store of value during government inflations. Argentine farmland is some of the world's most productive farmland... A hundred years ago, Argentina was "the breadbasket of Europe." Its agriculture and natural resources led it to become the world's 10th-wealthiest nation.

So what happened in the last 100 years? How could Argentina fall so far in that time? To me, the blame lies significantly with the government...

For nearly 100 years, Argentina has had bad politicians who consistently rang up large government debts while putting the people through excessive regulation/socialism... only to see this unsuccessful formula blow up on the people, over and over again.

Hopefully, our next 100 years in the U.S. will turn out better than Argentina's. But these days, it sure feels like the U.S. government wants to repeat Argentina's formula for failure – large debts, excessive regulation, and more socialist tendencies.

There is one thing we can do to protect our wealth. We can follow Eduardo... we can buy farms, real estate, and gold – REAL things that hold their value when the government goes too far.

Since the 1990s, Eduardo has built one of the world's finest portfolios of real estate. He has made his fortune by being patient for opportunities to appear... and then being bold and aggressive when the time is right.

Cresud manages about 2.5 million acres of farmland. About 1 million acres of this land is in productive use. It has about 66,000 in total cattle stock. About 64,000 are beef cattle stock and around 2,400 are dairy cows.

And Cresud is well-run and incredibly profitable. So what's not to like? There's one catch: The stock is expensive...

Cresud (CRESY)

Historically, the time to buy Cresud has been when the stock has been trading for less than book value. When Cresud shares bottomed in 2002... the stock was trading for around 0.8 times book value.

In 2014, shares traded for more than three times book value. No matter how fantastic the business is, that's too much to pay for the shares. Patience will pay off. At some point, shares will dip into buy range.

We recommend you put it on your watch list and buy it when it trades for less than book.

PART SEVEN

The Nine Most Important Things I'm Doing to Prepare for a Crisis in America

An Interview with Porter Stansberry

Porter note: In May 2014, I sat down for a lengthy interview about what steps I'd take personally to prepare for a financial crisis in America.

In the edited transcript that follows, you'll learn what I consider the nine most important steps for protecting your money, your assets, your safety, and your family.

———————●———————

Stansberry Research: Porter, you have been predicting a major crisis here in America for a few years now. I suspect most of our readers know that doesn't mean you think the world will end. But many of them may not be entirely sure about what you think is going to happen.

Porter Stansberry: First, I want to clarify that a major crisis is already going on in our country – and around the world, for that matter. Most people don't realize it. But a currency crisis has been ongoing in the U.S. dollar for years. All you need to do is look at the facts...

The U.S. dollar has lost roughly half of its purchasing power in the last 15 years. You need to spend nearly twice as much cash to purchase something as you had to pay in 1999 or 2000 for the same item. That's really not long ago. So this is a continual currency crisis that we're living in now. The real question people should be asking is whether it's likely to accelerate.

Stansberry Research: Is that where the signs are pointing?

Porter: It's common knowledge that the U.S. economy has an unsustainable debt load. And it's only getting worse. The easiest way for the government to get out of that debt is for the central bank to print a lot of money.

And that's what they're doing... How do we know? Because they're not hiding any of it. So it's only a matter of time until there's a significant loss of purchasing power. When everyday items get expensive, people are going to notice and become upset.

Stansberry Research: That sounds gloomy...

Porter: I'm not saying we'll experience a complete societal collapse. There are several different ways this could unfold. But one thing is for sure: We will have a major currency crisis on our hands soon. It could last a few days, a week, or much longer. But regardless... I'm not worried, personally. I'm confident in the steps I've taken to protect myself and my family.

While I don't ever want something like this to happen – it's going to hurt a lot of hard-working U.S. folks – I'm not going to let denial catch me unprepared. In a situation like this, some things you want to do are just logical.

For example, economies essentially shut down for relatively long periods of time during a currency crisis.

During the 2001-2002 crisis in Argentina, no banking was available at all for a period of about six weeks. There were no ATMs. There was no ability to write checks. There was nothing. The whole economy ground to a halt.

It became basically a barter system. There wasn't enough cash to drive all the transactions. If you didn't have the world's reserve currency – U.S. dollars – you couldn't buy anything. You had to trade for it.

I remember my business partners, whom I probably shouldn't mention by name, bought either a townhouse or an apartment, I forget. But they bought some real estate down there in the middle of that crisis. An attorney had to fly to Argentina to close the deal at a bank. The Argentine seller wanted $300,000 for a property that was worth more than $1 million... But he would only do the deal in U.S. dollars and in cash.

So they wired $300,000 down there, and the attorney pushed it across the table to the seller. The Argentine counted one stack of 100 bills, counted all the stacks, and passed the keys over to their attorney. And the deal was done. The Argentine put the cash in a briefcase and walked out the door. It was classic.

Most Americans have no concept that this type of situation could happen here. People forget that banks have very little cash on hand. The reserve ratio of the U.S. banking industry has been on a steady decline since World War II. So we're more and more at risk of a major bank run.

And let's be honest – being prepared for something like this just makes good common sense. How do you know that there won't be some computer virus that shuts down the power grid or causes banks to have errors? If 11 transformers blew up, the whole national power grid would fail. This wouldn't necessarily have to be the result of terrorism. It could just be a mistake.

A situation like this may not last long. They would probably be able to fix that in a couple days. But we could always face a situation where for a period of three to five days you don't have access to any kind of banking. So the first thing that I would urge people to do is to have **a safe place outside the bank to store a reasonable amount of currency, gold, and silver**... and believe it or not, also guns and ammunition.

Stansberry Research: When you talk about holding cash, are you referring to the U.S. dollar?

Porter: Yes, because the U.S. dollar still remains the world's reserve currency. Now if you really wanted to protect yourself, you could diversify easily. You could get some euros. I would maybe get some Canadian dollars. That seems to be a much safer alternative because it's a commodity-based currency.

The safe currencies are basically going to be the Swiss franc, the Singapore dollar, and the Canadian dollar. I imagine you would be safe with a healthy mix of any of those currencies.

Stansberry Research: Where exactly do you suggest storing it? In your house or a safety deposit box?

Porter: Well, I'm not going to tell you exactly where I keep my money... That wouldn't make it very safe, now would it?

All kidding aside, it's reasonably secure to keep these things in a safe somewhere in your house or on some piece of property you own. But make sure the safe is well-hidden. I wouldn't leave it in my closet.

And you don't have to spend a fortune on this kind of thing. A simple way to do this is to get a self-storage unit. They have 24-hour surveillance. And you use your own lock. Who's going to go looking in a self-storage unit for gold bullion? It's not going to happen. So you could just put a small safe in a self-storage unit and put a bunch of other junk on top of it.

So if somebody does happen to break into it, what are they going to see? Just junk. They're not going to find your bullion. Just make sure that you don't tell anyone where you've hidden your gold, and you pay your storage fees.

Another obviously cheap solution is burying it. You can rent a Bobcat for a day and bury anything you want. If you do that, be careful you don't run into power lines or sewer lines.

Some of this may sound a bit crazy, but it's crazier to be unprepared. The far more dangerous thing is not taking these precautions, right? You're not increasing your risk by taking a small amount of currency and bullion and pulling it out of the bank. You're actually reducing your risk.

Stansberry Research: It certainly can't hurt.

Porter: But really the gold standard is a Swiss passport. If you have all the money in the world and you want the ultimate bug-out plan, then get an apartment in Zurich and a Swiss passport. You can get that done for about $5 million.

Stansberry Research: Well that's great, but how many people can actually afford to do that?

Porter: Not many. Like I said, it's the gold standard. That's what I'm working for. But the important thing I want to get across is that you need to become less U.S.-dependent.

I'll give you another kind of extreme example. I have a friend who is the UN council of some tiny island nation in the pacific. Someplace I can't pronounce.

He gave the government there a quarter-million dollars or so, and they made him part of their UN staff. So he has a diplomatic passport that allows him to travel anywhere in the world.

Stansberry Research: So what could someone who isn't a millionaire do to become less U.S.-dependent?

Porter: It depends on where you live. I have a place in Miami. If I lived there full-time, I would get a bank account in the Bahamas with a safety deposit box. That would be a very easy solution for me. It's easy for me to transfer bullion and paper bills to those locations. If you live in the northeast, Canada is a great solution. Or if you live near the U.S/Mexico border, then you can do the same in Mexico.

The idea is just to diversify your savings in a way that would allow you to prosper even in the event of a breakdown of the U.S. banking system, whether that was due to a currency collapse or due to a technological failure or do to some kind of malfeasance. You know, maybe hackers break into your bank and steal all the money or something.

Stansberry Research: So just to reiterate, you think the most important things our readers can do in preparation for a currency crisis is having some of their assets outside a bank and becoming less U.S.-dependent...

Porter: Yes, but don't forget about having plenty of currency on hand. And that is especially true if you are traveling.

I've got a good story about that, by the way...

What would you say is generally associated with carrying large sums of cash? After all, it is very frowned upon in the world.

Stansberry Research: I don't know... Probably drugs or prostitution. Something illicit like that.

Porter: Right, it is very frowned upon in the world. But a lot of the older, very successful people I know simply think it's prudent to carry a large amount of cash.

So one senior newsletter writer I know very well always carries at least $100,000 in cash with him everywhere he goes, and it came in handy one time we were traveling in Argentina...

We were in the Salta Province in northwest Argentina, and it was about 7 o'clock at night. Once we got to where we were going, a close colleague of mine picked up a call on his cell phone from his wife. She said the worst thing you could possibly imagine hearing, "Our daughter has viral meningitis, and she's not going to live through the night. You have to come as soon as you can."

So think about that...

It's 7 o'clock at night. You're in the middle of nowhere in rural Argentina. And your daughter's not going to live until the morning, what do you do?

What would any good friend do? You pick up the phone and call the concierge at the hotel back in Buenos Aires. You say, "My colleague's daughter is dying back in the U.S. We need a Gulfstream here ASAP, and we need to get my friend to the hospital back in the U.S. as quickly as is humanly possible."

And the concierge says, "The plane will leave in 45 minutes." He hangs up and makes it happen.

The plane is in the air. The pilot calls me. "Listen, buddy, we're in the air, but I'm turning the plane around right now unless you can assure me that there's $85,000 in cash when we land."

"How about we wire it to your bank in the morning?" I ask.

"No can do," he says. "We need it on the tarmac."

There are 10 of us in the group. Now, it's 9 o'clock at night, and of course, we're still in the middle of nowhere, Argentina. "Hey, anybody got $85,000 I can borrow?" I ask.

That's not a made-up story. That really happened. I was there, and there was no substitute for having $100,000 in cash. My cash-carrying friend saved the day. Without this cash on hand, there's no way this could have happened.

Stansberry Research: Was his daughter OK?

Porter: It's a long story, but eventually he got there at around 2 p.m. the next day. And fortunately, his daughter survived.

Stansberry Research: Wow.

Porter: But yeah, it was unpleasant. Anyway, things can happen... especially if you're traveling. Often when those things happen, there is no substitute for cash. A lot of times when I'm on my boat in the Bahamas and we're running low on fuel, we'll find an island with a tiny dock... like you'd see on a Microsoft screensaver, you know?

There's a little tiny island with one dock and a Texaco fuel pump. You know there's no way you can use a credit card because the cellular system's never working. So unless you have cash, it's a no-go.

Stansberry Research: Those are some amazing stories. It really sounds like something straight out of a movie, but I'm glad his daughter was OK.

Porter: Trust me, it's not something you want to go through. My son got very sick and was hospitalized for a while. It puts things in perspective. Nothing's more important than your family's health.

But people don't think about that sort of thing. If something were to happen – even if you couldn't go to a pharmacy for a few days – do you think people are prepared for that?

No way, nobody even considers what it would be like if you couldn't get medicine or go to the grocery store for a week or a month at a time. If you require medication for your health...

Stansberry Research: Or your kids...

Porter: Right, especially if you're a diabetic or something like that. Believe me, those things will be the most important things to have stockpiled.

Stansberry Research: Even basic antibiotics.

Porter: Yes, it's smart to have a secret stash of antibiotics and first-aid supplies. I don't want you to think I'm a "doomsday prepper"... I'm not.

I don't think it makes any sense to believe you can live in a hole in the ground for a year. But I definitely believe in having the resources and the ability to take care of yourself and your family for a seven- to 10-day emergency period... and ideally having the wherewithal to be able to leave the country if the crisis were to get worse.

Stansberry Research: It's always smart to have an exit strategy...

Porter: Definitely. I would have an escape plan, not a hole in the ground. But in any case, it's reasonable to keep a seven- to 10-day supply of cash, medicines, food, water, and guns and ammunition. There's no doubt that the social order in our country could break down.

Stansberry Research: But if the social order seriously begins to break down during a currency crisis and things get dangerous, what can our readers to do, other than trying to get out of the United States? I mean, that might not be an option for everybody.

Porter: Right, it probably isn't. I can tell you which neighborhoods you don't want to go into. And I think we all know where those places are.

Stansberry Research: Don't head to Baltimore?

Porter: Don't head to Baltimore. There's a reason why we built a 12-foot wall around our building, right?

I saw a recent infographic yesterday in Chicago that showed the demographics of the city. It showed how the very poor had expanded out into the suburbs in Chicago, and the very rich had become more and more isolated in the center of the city on the shore.

I would try to find a way to get to any of the 50 or so places in the country that have real concentrations of wealth.

You know those signs that say, "We accept EBT"?

Stansberry Research: Yeah, those are places that take food stamps, right?

Porter: Exactly. Those are the areas you want to avoid.

Stansberry Research: I get what you're saying. But couldn't the really wealthy areas become a target? If you're in the center of the city with all the wealth but surrounded on all sides by neighborhoods where people are collecting food stamps, is that really a good idea?

Porter: Yeah, in fact it is. That's where I want to be. The rich people are going to take care of themselves. I remember when Hurricane Katrina hit New Orleans. The people living in one really wealthy neighborhood, Audubon Place, flew in a team of Israeli mercenaries on a private jet and put their whole neighborhood on lock down. Nobody came in or out.

Stansberry Research: Not a bad private security force to have in a pinch.

Porter: Exactly. So if you asked me whether I'd rather be in Compton or Beverly Hills, I'm going take Beverly Hills. And this type of advice applies to everyone. If you have the option to live in a big house in a transitioning neighborhood or an apartment in a wealthy area, it's safer to choose the apartment every time.

Stansberry Research: I was just suggesting that maybe you would leave the city and go out into a more rural area?

Porter: If you study past breakdowns of society – the riots in '68, for example, here in Baltimore or the ones in Detroit – the rioters always burn their own stores.

And just think about it. People out in Baltimore County are armed to the teeth. You don't want to go there.

Stansberry Research: Yeah, you probably don't want to test your mettle against a bunch of angry farmer's with shotguns.

Since we are on the subject, any other worst-case-scenario precautions? What about generators or anything like that? I know you're not a prepper, but being without power for a week or a month during a crisis seems like it could make things worse.

Porter: Listen, if you can afford it, a generator is always a smart idea. Plus, they are great for things like hurricanes, blizzards, or even just Baltimore's power grid. I've got backup generators and all that, but...

Stansberry Research: Do they run on natural gas?

Porter: They run on propane. I've got really big propane tanks. But they're only going to keep that generator going for a maximum of seven to 10 days before it runs out of fuel. So I don't really think that generators are the answer except for in a very short-term scenario, like a hurricane or a power outage.

Like I said, if there's a crisis that's going to be longer than a week, I'm not staying... I'm leaving.

Stansberry Research: Got it.

Porter: And so I think the best thing you could have is a boat or the ability to get to Canada or to Mexico or somewhere of your choice. But I don't think of this is a currency crisis precaution... more like an end-of-the-world thing. Most of the precautions people should take are really just common sense kind of things

Stansberry Research: Like what?

Porter: I'd recommend like once a year maybe go through a folder in your safe that has your critical documents: birth certificates (the originals), your passport, your insurance policies, etc. All those critical documents should be in the same place. I do it on my birthday.

I also have a cover letter on my folder that tells my wife where all of our assets are, what the account numbers and passwords are. All that stuff.

And you might say that's a security vulnerability. It is. But if they've already broken in and forced me to open my bullion safe, I got bigger problems than the fact that they now have all my account numbers and passwords.

Stansberry Research: What about specific cash holdings? I know you said to have cash on hand, but people always wonder exactly how much cash they actually need. How much should I have in cash?

Porter: A good thing is to have enough cash so that you can pay all your bills for 30 days. Figure out what your requirement of cash is for 30 days and assume that you can't write a check or go to the ATM machine. I don't think you have to be paranoid to know you don't want to end up in a situation where you don't have any money.

Stansberry Research: And gold or silver? How much gold should people keep on hand?

Porter: I think it makes sense to hold, you know, 5% to 10% percent of your net worth in precious metals. And whether it's gold or silver really doesn't make any difference. I would look at the silver-to-gold ratio, and I would allocate the value.

Traditionally, the "gold to silver" ratio has been as low as 16 to 1. Meaning the price of an ounce of gold cost 16 times more than the price of an ounce of silver.

In recent years, the ratio has been much higher than 16 to 1. If it's above 50, I would probably buy silver. Meaning if gold is 50 times more expensive than silver, then I think silver's cheap relative to gold. If the silver ratio is 25, then I would buy gold.

And what I do is very simple. Every year in January, when I'm done paying my taxes and paying off my Christmas gifts, I take the money left over from the previous year, call up my broker, and put it into gold bullion. I've never sold a single ounce of it. And to tell you the honest-to-God truth, I don't even know exactly how much I own. I just keep putting it in a pile, so to speak.

I just don't keep all that much money in my checking account. Anyone who reads my newsletter knows I don't recommend keeping much money in your checking account. I keep far more of my assets in my brokerage account.

Stansberry Research: Do you have the physical, paper shares?

Porter: No, I don't bother with any of that.

Stansberry Research: You're not worried that all of that just might disappear one day?

Porter: I'm not worried about it.

Stansberry Research: All that money in your brokerage account?

Porter: I have a significant portion of my net worth in physical things – houses, farms, gold, and real estate. I've got a business that's worth a lot. So if the worst were to come, I'm sure I'd be OK. Henry Ford has a great quote that your only real security in life is the people that you know and the skills that you have. So I don't live in fear.

But for people who are retired, these are much more important questions. Those folks want to make sure that they understand who controls the title to things. And if they're going to own stocks like IBM and Hershey forever, it might make a lot of sense to demand the paper shares and put them in the vault. It can't hurt.

Stansberry Research: If you don't plan on selling them any time soon...

Porter: Yes, and in fact, that might be a really useful thing for some people. A lot of people have a really hard time just sitting still and hanging on to financial assets because you can just go trade them any time you want. So if you find yourself having that problem of not being able to hold onto things for the long term, then get the paper stock.

Stansberry Research: I've been thinking about doing that myself lately. I have some stock that I don't plan on selling for at least a decade or two.

Porter: That's smart then. It can also be very comforting.

Stansberry Research: Yes... until you start worrying if there's a fire.

Porter: Well, I'm sure there's a corporate registry if that were to happen. I believe there's an account somewhere that shows that you own a certain percentage of the shares.

*[**Editor's note:** It is possible to recover your stock if your physical shares are lost, stolen, or otherwise damaged. Typically, you must contact the company's transfer agent, and it will help you begin the process of recovering your shares. You will have to give the details surrounding the loss of the shares, as well as provide some information to verify that you are indeed the rightful owner.]*

Stansberry Research: Speaking of stocks, Porter, what kind of investments should people make to protect themselves and some of their money during a currency crisis?

Porter: The important thing you want to do is make sure that your savings are being held in an asset that can manage an environment of sharply rising prices. So the most important thing for you to do is to not own bonds, especially long-term bonds. There is a mania in the bond market. People have responded to this global uncertainty by buying fixed income and that has forced the yield way down on these bonds.

First, it's important for people to know that when the price of a bond goes up, the yield goes down. So you'll see bonds now, low-quality, risky bonds – not investment-grade bonds – trading at prices way above par so that their yields are actually less than 5%. It's absolutely insane to purchase these low-quality bonds. You know through history that more than 5% of these bonds are likely to default.

If you bought a broad portfolio of these bonds, over time you would make nothing. Meanwhile, over a 10-year period, the purchasing power of the dollar is going to decline by 15% or 20%, even if we're wrong about any kind of crisis.

The simple reality is that you're going to lose money in real terms with these bonds, but most people don't understand that.

Something else you want to be cautious about is life-insurance policies. If you have an insurance policy you've been paying for a long time and the death benefit isn't likely to be paid until 20-25 years from now... the real value of that payout is nothing compared with the value that you are giving the insurance companies. The insurance companies got pre-inflation dollars, and they only have to pay out post-inflation dollars.

Instead of buying life insurance, buy the life-insurance company instead, right? If it can afford to pay out those benefits, it's not doing it for free. It's getting something more out of the deal. So watch out for bonds, especially long-term bonds. Watch out for insurance policies.

Stansberry Research: What about specific types of companies that you should own?

Porter: A lot of people want to buy mining companies as a shield against inflation. They think, "I'll go buy a gold mine and if inflation drives up the price of gold, I'll be protected."

But the reality is these companies don't tend to perform well during periods of inflation. It costs them more to replace their production than they're able to earn selling their gold.

Think about this for a second... say a gold mine has $100 million of gold in it. And you buy it with today's dollars. You're only going to get paid for your gold in the inflated currency. Now, you'll get paid more for it. But in terms of real purchasing power, there's no great increase.

And what happens when the $100 million is gone when all the gold has been produced?

Stansberry Research: There's nothing left.

Porter: Exactly. You own nothing.

So in 10 years, you've got nothing but some inflated dollars back. Meanwhile what really happens is the manager of the gold mine says, "We need to find a new resource." He takes all the money he made selling the gold and buys another hugely expensive mine. And the shareholder gets nothing.

Stansberry Research: What about asset-rich companies that aren't mines or resource-producing companies? Something like a real estate trust or something along those lines.

Porter: What you really want to do is focus on what we call "beachfront property." Not literally beachfront property... but the best assets in the world. You want to focus on what we call "Trophy Assets" that can't be replicated.

The key is you've got to make sure you don't pay too much for it because the prices of these asset prices will soar in anticipation of inflation. And we've already seen that in real estate. The great example of this is the Empire State Building went public in 2013.

Stansberry Research: Wow, I didn't know that.

Porter: Yeah. So think about this for a second. Are the folks who own the Empire State Building likely to know more or less about the real estate market than the general public?

So when you see that kind of thing you have to be very, very cautious. Likewise, the best portfolio ever assembled of corporate real estate was a business called Equity Office Properties.

A famous Chicagoan named Sam Zell built that business over a 30-year period. Sam is one of the people we quote warning about the potential for the loss of the world reserve currency. And Sam sold all of his real estate in January 2007. He sold the company he spent his life assembling, and he did it because people's expectations of inflation were even greater than the risks of inflation.

And so you have to warn people that this Trophy Asset strategy is well-known and you have to be cautious about when you decide to follow it. Our bias is you should try to buy these things when they're trading at half of whatever their estimated asset value is.

And you're only going to get those opportunities during certain rare crisis moments. You have to watch them all and be ready to acquire them at the appropriate time.

But **the best way to protect yourself from inflation is by owning your own asset-light business**. Just for a moment, imagine what would happen to our publishing company if the dollar fell by 50% overnight.

Stansberry Research: You probably wouldn't have to pay me as much.

Porter: Exactly... all of my costs would fall in real terms because all of my labor costs would be decimated. The amounts we're paying you guys in real terms would fall in half. Meanwhile what are my real asset costs? I have almost none. I'd send everybody a note and saying I can't afford postage and printing anymore, so if you can't get your newsletter online, you can't have it.

Stansberry Research: Not a bad business to be in...

Porter: That's what I want people to understand. Cutting a few costs would eliminate all of the damage of inflation to my business. And it would be great because it would reduce my labor costs tremendously.

So for folks who have the wherewithal to structure their own businesses in an asset-light basis, that's the very best way to deal with inflation.

If you can't have your own business that's asset light, you need to look in the stock market for businesses that have that characteristic. We call these "capital efficient" companies. I've written volumes and volumes and volumes about this.

We recommended Hershey in my *Investment Advisoy* in December 2007, which was pretty much the worst possible time that you could imagine to buy stock, right?

It was right in front of 2008, and we didn't stop out of it – meaning it didn't drop 25% from when we purchased... which would have triggered us to sell from our portfolio. This simple fact alone tells you how resilient that business is.

I studied the price per ounce of chocolate versus the price per ounce of gold over a 100-year period. And it turns out that Hershey's chocolate bars were a better hedge against inflation than gold was. I think that's a really valuable secret.

It just goes to show you that there's a mindset out there that the only way to protect yourself against inflation is gold. That mindset is wrong. There are many consumer products that people value more than gold.

And you know I would put medicine in that category. I would put oil in that category, and I would put beloved consumer goods like Coca-Cola and chocolate in that category.

Stansberry Research: All right. Well I think we got good stuff. I think we have some really solid advice that our readers can use to their advantage.

Porter: Before you go, I just want to make one thing clear. I want people to know they shouldn't feel paranoid or scared. What's happening now has been going on for 50 years. There's an easy, sensible strategy that will make you wealthier than you otherwise would be so long as you understand the forces at play and prepare accordingly.

Stansberry Research: Thanks again for your time, Porter.

Porter: Thank you.

Summary:
Porter's Nine Keys to
Survive a Currency Crisis

1. Have a safe place outside the bank to store a reasonable amount of currency, gold, and silver.

2. Become less "U.S.-dependent" by holding assets overseas and/or having a plan to evacuate to another country.

3. Keep a seven- to 10-day supply of cash, medicines, food, water, and guns and ammunition.

4. Find a way to get to any of the 50 or so places in the country that have real concentrations of wealth.

5. Review your critical documents (birth certificate, passport, etc.) once a year.

6. Do not hold bonds.

7. Be cautious buying life insurance.

8. Own your own "asset-light" business.

9. Focus your stock investing on "Trophy Assets" and capital-efficient businesses.

PART EIGHT

How to Own the
World's Trophy Assets

Chapter 1

The Most Profitable and Stable Form of Leveraged Investing

In mid-2007, private-equity firm Blackstone Group went public in a huge and highly publicized initial stock offering.

The public was so eager to buy the stock, bankers were able to push the value of the firm to nearly $40 billion. Blackstone had roughly 1,500 employees at the time. According to the stock market, these employees were worth $26.6 million each, making them the most valuable people in the history of capitalism... at least, for a few months.

Due to the outrageous valuation and the incredible hype, the stock soon cratered. It fell from more than $30 per share to less than $5 in a little more than a year. We wrote at the time of the initial public offering (IPO) that Blackstone's shares were not safe. We saw the IPO as one of the most obvious signs of a general stock market peak...

> Chief Executive Stephen Schwarzman and his partner Peter Peterson started this company in 1985 with $400,000. They've worked hard for 22 years. And they're no dummies. They've seen a top in the credit markets before... and this time they're cashing out.
> – *The Stansberry Digest, June 17, 2007*

The Blackstone IPO turned out to be the metaphoric bell ringing at the top of the credit/housing/stock market bubble of 2004-2008. Within only a few weeks of the IPO, the credit markets began to crater, making it harder and more expensive for private-equity firms like Blackstone to get the financing they needed for their deals. Within a few months, credit was simply not available at any price. The stock's share price collapsed.

It would be easy to write off the success of the private-equity funds in the 1990s and early 2000s as simply an aberration – part of the excesses created by a credit-fueled bull market. Except that Blackstone survived the crash.

Blackstone didn't just survive... It prospered and became even larger, in terms of assets under management. At more than $32 billion in market cap, investors value the firm at around $33 million per employee in 2014. With $265 billion in assets under management and $6.9 billion in revenue in 2013, these folks are still incredibly good at making money.

Blackstone's survival, even more than its earlier success, argues its strategy is no fluke. Its acumen is real.

Whatever your particular opinion about Blackstone's future is, you can't deny the private-equity model has proven to be the most profitable and stable form of leveraged investing. In the Securities and Exchange Commission filings that accompanied the IPO, Blackstone disclosed that, while still a private company, its co-founder Stephen Schwarzman earned more than $300 million a year in compensation.

These numbers and the success of so many of Blackstone's investments raise the question...

How do they do it?

How does Blackstone make so much money with so few people? And what can we learn from its success?

Chapter 2

How Private Equity Works

Private-equity firms are mysterious and often portrayed in the liberal media as sinister. Few investors understand how they work.

But everyone knows one thing: They make a lot of money. *On average, Blackstone's clients have earned about 22% annually from their investments in Blackstone's private-equity funds since the firm's inception in the 1980s.*

That's after accounting for the firm's 2% annual management fee and the 20% of profits it takes as its carried interest.

The clients are happy to pay those fees because that 22% rate of return doubles their money in a little more than three years. These kinds of returns aren't normally available to equity investors. Even Warren Buffett, the greatest investor who ever lived, has only averaged about 20% over the long term.

How do they do it?

Simple: They borrow money. Private-equity firms use other people's money to buy assets. Then they use the earnings from those assets to pay back the debt. After a few years, they're left owning the assets outright and can sell them back to the public via a new IPO. In short... they engineer deals that enable them to transform debt into equity.

That might sound complicated, but it's not.

It's essentially the same thing that mom-and-pop real estate investors do all the time. They buy a house, putting only 20% down in equity. They get a bank to loan them the balance, using the asset (the house) as collateral. Then they find a renter to pay the interest and the principal (by renting the house).

After a while – usually seven to 10 years – the mortgage is gone. The owners, who only paid 20% of the initial cost, are able to sell the property to a new buyer for more than they paid, resulting in a huge gain.

Private-equity firms do the same thing, using stocks instead of houses.

Like real estate investors, they start by searching for assets that are "diamonds in the rough" – companies that are managing their assets poorly and/or have seen their shares badly mispriced by the market.

Then, using good contacts and relationships with the major commercial and investment banks, they raise colossal amounts of credit, borrowing billions to buy the companies they target. A lot of the big takeover deals you see written about in the papers are private-equity deals. A typical private-equity fund will buy around 20 different companies over seven years.

But… chances are good that you've never been invited to invest in a private-equity fund.

These pools of capital typically only serve very high net-worth individuals and large institutions, like sovereign-wealth funds, pension funds, and insurance companies.

To see how a private-equity deal really works, from start to finish, let's look at an actual deal…

Back in 2006, Richard Kinder, the CEO of Kinder Morgan (NYSE: KMI), the huge natural gas and oil pipeline company, was frustrated with his company's share price.

The firm had added billions in assets, via a new pipeline constructed under the Rocky Mountains. Yet the stock market didn't seem to notice. Kinder told his investors on a conference call in April 2006 that, at that current price, he'd like to own a lot more of the company. (He held 18% at the time.)

He meant what he said. He called his bankers at Goldman Sachs, who organized a group of private-equity funds (led by the Carlyle Group) to buy the company for $15 billion. To raise the money, the Carlyle Group tapped the banks it had worked with over many years. Since Rich Kinder already owned 18% of the company, the private-equity firms borrowed something on the order of $10 billion.

Nothing really changed about the company, its employees, or its management team. Rich Kinder is one of the true titans of the energy industry. A bunch of guys from New York weren't going to tell him how to do his job better.

But by only putting up $3 billion in equity to buy the company... the private-equity fund was positioning itself to make a windfall return. That is, it invested $3 billion to get a business that was already worth $13 billion, not including Kinder's stake.

The company – not the private-equity funds – then spent the next few years paying down its debts and growing its pipelines. By the end of 2009, the long-term debt was down to only $2.7 billion. And in early 2011, the stock was again sold to the public. Investors paid $30 a share, valuing the business at $21 billion.

The private-equity firms took $3 billion and turned it into roughly $15 billion in a little less than six years. Richard Kinder ended up with 30% of the company, which he kept. And the private-equity investors made five times their money. Plus, the company paid them roughly $1 billion a year in dividends along the way.

Look at the math: The private-equity firms bought a company from other investors worth $13 billion (with $3 billion of their cash and shares and $10 billion in bank debt). Then, thanks to growing earnings and a few acquisitions, they paid themselves roughly $6 billion in dividends (which doubled their money) before selling the entity back to the public for $21 billion.

Did you follow what happened? The answer is, almost nothing changed in terms of the company or its operations. The only thing that changed was the firm's capital structure. **A lot of debt was added and this capital flowed through the company and into the hands of the shareholders**.

It's a great deal, eh? Too bad we can't invest the same way, right?

Well... what if we could?

— Chapter 3 —

Private-Equity-Like Stocks

We have a few obvious ways to invest in private-equity deals. The simplest thing to do is buy the private-equity firms, many of which went public following Blackstone's 2007 IPO.

In fact, the stocks of private-equity companies like Blackstone Group (NYSE: BX) and Kohlberg Kravis Roberts (NYSE: KKR) are some of our favorite equities in the market. Thanks to the Federal Reserve's loose-money policies, they're in their "sweet spot."

They have nearly unlimited access to cheap capital, thanks to falling interest rates and the increasing money supply. This allows them to finance bigger and bigger deals – or in Blackstone's case, unload assets at rich multiples to their original prices.

And as the world's central banks continue to create trillions of dollars of paper money, private-equity firms gather more and more assets.

To take advantage of private-equity deals, you could also buy the shares of the companies private-equity firms are selling back to the public. The firms typically hold their stakes in these companies for several years. Often enough, these stocks perform well because they're highly leveraged, well-managed, and pay big dividends.

But a third way to invest in private-equity deals holds even more promise...

There is a group of companies whose assets are so valuable that they always have access to the credit markets. **We call them "trophy assets."**

These companies own one-of-a-kind assets. When managed the right way, they give public market investors the same high returns as private-equity investors because they can be safely leveraged to produce high returns on equity. While we wouldn't recommend investing in highly leveraged stocks in most cases... there are some important exceptions.

Some assets are of such high quality, they always have access to debt financing.

For example, take the most valuable mine in the world – the Grasberg complex in Papua, Indonesia.

Discovered in the late 1930s and developed by the Rockefeller family in the 1960s, the mining district began producing copper, gold, and silver in the early 1970s. In 2014, the mine is still the world's largest source of copper (averaging 1 billion pounds a year over the past five years) and gold (averaging 1.6 million ounces a year over the past five years).

The mine is so valuable, its eventual discovery was among the motivations that led the Japanese to invade the South Pacific. Likewise, when the Rockefellers' interest in the mine was threatened in the 1960s, the U.S. government engineered a civil war in Indonesia. The coup included one of the largest mass killing sprees in history, which followed a CIA-orchestrated revolution in September 1965.

A reliable death toll number has never been published, but eyewitnesses claim at least 1 million people were murdered in Indonesia. The number of floating corpses seriously impeded the country's river traffic. One of the first major acts of the new government was to annex Papua and take control of the mine.

Despite its bloody political origins, the mine itself is a stupendous human achievement. It sits among the highest mountain peaks in the world (more than 14,000 feet high) in one of the most remote places on Earth. Grasberg is a gigantic open-pit mine, with a mile-wide crater, which can be seen from space.

The facility also includes the world's largest milling equipment, which can process 240,000 metric tons of ore per day. The ore is sent via a slurry pipeline that runs more than 70 miles through the jungle to a seaport built to serve the mine.

Grasberg is a global trophy asset, perhaps the single-greatest trophy asset in the world.

Ownership is split between the Indonesian government (which controls 10%) and the public investors of global mining giant Freeport-McMoRan (NYSE: FCX), which owns 90%. The company estimates the mine still contains 30 billion pounds of copper, 30 million ounces of gold, and 113 million ounces of silver.

Now, you should know that Freeport-McMoRan has found itself in the midst of some hot-button issues, including a labor strike in 2011. And as recently as 2014, the company is mired in a spat with the Indonesian government over taxes. But the assets are there, and Freeport-McMoRan owns 90% of them.

Investors willing to buy at the right price and ride out the volatility will do well. To its credit, company management has done a fantastic job diversifying into some other high-potential areas, including huge investments in the oilfields deep below the Gulf of Mexico.

But the company's real assets are in the Grasberg mine. The gold alone would be worth around $35 billion at today's prices. Given the copper and silver resource in the ore, the gold could certainly be mined for free.

Interestingly, though... the company's market cap is only $30 billion. The discount to the company's obvious asset value isn't unusual. In fact, Freeport-McMoRan is one of the more volatile stocks we regularly follow. The value of its assets changes slowly. (In general, the value rises thanks to the impact of inflation.) But its share price bounces all around.

For example, in 2008, Freeport-McMoRan shares fell from $60 all the way down to almost $10 – a collapse of almost 80%. You can bet nothing changed about the Grasberg mine during that year. All that copper, gold, and silver was still sitting there, roasting under the equatorial sun.

Folks who claim that the stock market is perfectly efficient... that there are never important discrepancies between the price of a stock and the value of the underlying asset... should spend some time watching this stock. It often shows huge discrepancies between share price and asset value.

And as you'll see in the next chapter, that's exactly what we're looking for...

Chapter 4

To Maximize Your Returns, Buy Right

To replicate the returns of private equity, our strategy is simply to buy the highest-quality assets in the world – assets that can safely carry a lot of debt – when those assets are trading at a broad discount to both their historic valuation and their proven tangible asset value.

In essence, **we want to buy the Hope Diamond... but only at a cubic zirconia-like price**. The discounted price alone assures us of a good return over time. But there's something else that will help us make even more money... leverage. The quality of the assets these kinds of companies hold allows them to safely employ a lot of debt, which greatly boosts returns.

Take MGM Resorts International (NYSE: MGM), for example. The company owns most of the Las Vegas strip, including half of CityCenter, a $9 billion hotel and casino development.

CityCenter was at one point the largest privately financed development in the history of the United States.

MGM owns a host of similar, one-of-a-kind properties in the world's leading gambling cities, including Macau, the only place in China where gambling is legal.

According to the company's accountants, its properties are worth "only" $14 billion. It's important to realize that these balance sheet valuations almost always significantly understate the actual current market value because most of these assets are kept on the books at their acquisition cost.

MGM's assets may be worth more than the $14 billion accounting "acquisition cost." MGM's assets include nearly 1.2 million square feet of casinos on the Vegas strip, another roughly 470,000 square feet of casinos elsewhere in the U.S., and 50% of the 300,000-plus square feet of MGM Macau.

Consider that in 2009 (in the middle of one of the biggest Vegas recessions in history), MGM sold its Treasure Island casino on the strip for nearly $14,000 per square foot. At those prices, MGM's Vegas strip properties are worth more than $15 billion all by themselves... you get the Macau property and the other U.S. property for nearly nothing.

Against its assets, MGM has borrowed $13 billion. For many companies, this would be too much debt... But MGM can easily afford the $600 million it paid last year in interest because the quality of its assets is so high.

In a few years, the company could pay down these debts, leaving investors with massive increases to equity. Now, the company may not do this. It could buy additional assets, instead (more likely). **But the point is, as long as interest rates are so low, the company gets to use this capital for next to nothing, which means its shareholders are going to get rich**.

It's the same thing private-equity investors do: They convert debt into profit.

So... how much should you pay to own almost all of the Las Vegas strip... and a bunch of other first-class properties in the world's gambling centers? How much would you pay for the equity, knowing its growth potential? Well... you might be surprised.

The stock fell from almost $100 per share to less than $10 during the crisis of 2008. Again, nothing much changed about its business. Its hotels are still one-of-a-kind. They are still full of gamblers. And last time I checked, Vegas is still there.

What changes, as you know, is the market's appreciation of these assets. But the assets themselves don't change much. They can always be used as collateral. They always turn a profit. MGM proved this by surviving the crisis.

— Chapter 5 —

Why This Kind of Investing Is So Profitable

Trophy asset investing is special for two reasons.

First, unlike a lot of other investments, you can know what these assets are worth because they always carry a premium value to comparable properties thanks to their prized nature.

We could spend years trying to figure out what, say, Google, is really worth. And we might never figure it out... But with companies that hold trophy assets, we can know with tremendous confidence that the underlying assets are always going to be worth a lot.

And that brings us to the second key part of the strategy: **high returns on equity, thanks to leverage.**

Financing for these kinds of assets is always available. That enables the companies that own these assets to use a lot of debt to increase their annual returns on equity, which is exactly the same thing that private-equity firms do. That's why the ongoing profits from holding these stocks can be so high. This is what gives us our biggest advantage.

Private-equity firms earn high returns by taking big risks. They manage those risks by playing an active role in managing the businesses they buy.

Since we're public investors and don't have a voice in the day-to-day operations of the companies we own, we can only invest in highly leveraged companies when we are certain the underlying assets are of the highest quality. By limiting ourselves to watching only the highest-quality companies, we greatly reduce our risk.

Here's a list of stocks that qualify as bona-fide trophy properties...

Name	Ticker	ROE %	Discount or Premium to Tangible Assets
Chesapeake	CHK	4%	-65%
Transocean	RIG	11%	-64%
Cresud	CRESY	-38%	-57%
Freeport-McMoRan	FCX	11%	-54%
Posco	PKX	3%	-53%
Calpine	CPN	10%	-46%
MGM	MGM	4%	-38%
Teekay LNG Partners	TGP	11%	-23%
Kinder Morgan	KMI	10%	-21%
Rio Tinto	RIO	13%	-14%
BHP	BHP	18%	2%
Boston Properties	BXP	6%	4%
Plum Creek Timber	PCL	13%	29%
Royal Gold	RGLD	3%	37%
Silver Wheaton	SLW	9%	49%
Cheniere Energy	LNG	-147%	50%
Potash	POT	15%	60%
Walt Disney *	DIS	17%	88%
Union Pacific	UNP	23%	106%
Hershey *	HSY	58%	260%

Evaluation uses total assets rather than tangible assets due to brand value
Data Source: Bloomberg
Data as of November 3, 2014

As you can see, most of these firms are in the natural resource industry. There was a huge bull market in resources for 14 years. Many modern investors don't believe these "Hope Diamonds" will ever trade at cubic-zirconia prices. But trust us... they will.

As a general rule of thumb, **we want to wait to buy these stocks when we can get at least a 25% discount from tangible asset value.** (There are a few exceptions, which we'll explain.) The larger the discount, the more interested we become. Keep in mind, 25% is a broad guideline, not an automatic "buy" trigger.

When we see one of these companies trading at that size discount, we must evaluate the individual stock before making specific buying recommendations. In some circumstances, we may demand an even larger discount...

This kind of investing is a little like buying real estate. As good real estate investors know, you're buying "location" – the quality of the property – not countertops or flooring. All of the cosmetic stuff can be fixed.

We will focus on two key variables: **First, we need to understand a lot about the history of the stock price relative to the value of the tangible assets the company owns**.

Obviously, we want to buy these assets at the biggest possible discount. But in some cases, that's not possible. So *we need to make sure that in the context of the company's trading history, we're buying at the right time.*

Second, we have to make sure nothing is fundamentally wrong with the assets we're buying. To make sure they're not impaired, we look at the current return on equity. This gives us a good indication about the future rate of return. Ideally, we want to see annual returns on equity of 20% or more... as our plan is to make about 20% annually.

To do that, we've got to buy the world's best assets when they trade at a significant discount. Leverage will help us too, as it will ramp up the returns on equity.

The hard part is, the companies with the best annualized return on equity are normally going to trade at a big premium to asset value. We're looking for outliers... stocks with great assets and a great return on equity but that trade at huge discounts to asset value.

Looking at the summary table above, you can immediately see several companies trading at a substantial discount to tangible asset value. But to decide if any represent good investing opportunities, we start by comparing the size of the discount to the return on equity. That shows you where you can get the best quality and the biggest discount.

Below, you'll find a comparison of the individual stocks in this report across two variables: discount to asset value (price) and return on equity (quality).

This chart compares return on equity to the discount (or premium) of each stock compared to the value of the company's tangible assets. Companies above the trend line have a higher return on equity than expected, given their price.

As you can see, the highest-quality companies, like Hershey (NYSE: HSY), trade at the highest price (premium to asset value). The intangible nature of Hershey's brand makes it unlikely the company will ever trade at a discount to tangible assets.

Otherwise, there are no obvious outliers. That's OK. Great opportunities don't come around every day. That's why we've built this screen... to monitor the companies with the world's most prized assets so we can buy them when the market loses sight of what they're really worth. You can't always buy the Hope Diamond at a cubic-zirconia price. But when you can, it's an exceptional opportunity...

Just remember: With this kind of investing, you make your money based on when you buy. As a general rule... Buy these stocks when they trade for less than 75% of asset value (said another way, at a 25% discount to asset value) and when a confirmed uptrend is in place.

Waiting on the trend to turn in the right direction is important because we've seen in the past that the market participants will often dump these asset-rich companies at prices that don't make any sense. We want to wait for that irrational selling to subside and buy when the shares are on their way back up... as opposed to trying to catch a "falling knife."

Doing so will produce profits of more than 20% a year. And the best part is... it's not hard. All you have to do is follow a few of the world's best assets. Then buy them when they're trading at huge discounts to their underlying values.

PART NINE

Porter Stansberry's Crash Course on How to Become a Better Investor

— Chapter 1 —

The Fed's Biggest Fear
Should Be Yours, Too

In June 2014, I sat down to write a nine-day series of lessons for individual investors.

Each day in our *Stansberry Digest* e-letter, I discussed one critical investment lesson, with the goal of showing readers how to make big returns while taking small risks.

These essays covered topics such as...

- The seven best "one click" funds to manage your portfolio

- The only sector I hope my children invest in

- Four steps to consistently beat the market

- The trick to safely producing triple-digit winners in the market

They became "instant classics" with our readers.

Part Nine of *America 2020* contains all nine essays. It won't take long to read them. You might not agree with my ideas. But I promise they will encourage you to think about investing in a new way... and the knowledge you'll gain will last your entire life.

(**Please note**: The following essays were written in June 2014. So any specific numbers or opportunities they contain may be out of date. These classic essays are simply meant as a learning tool for how to be a better, smarter, and more sophisticated investor.)

———————●———————

We'll start off our nine-day series with a topic that I bet will surprise you... a review of the world's best exchange-traded funds (ETFs).

I'm going to give you seven well-run ETFs that you can buy safely and enjoy their outstanding investment performance... even if you know absolutely nothing about investing and you have no desire to learn. This is for all of our readers who don't want to manage their own assets, but want better-than-reasonable returns on their savings.

ETFs are investment funds that can hold any of a variety of assets (like stocks, but also bonds or commodities). The key feature is their shares trade on public stock exchanges, so you can buy shares of them just as you would shares of an individual company's stock.

What we're looking for in our list of the seven best ETFs isn't necessarily diversification or the cheapest possible fees... We're looking for funds that help investors succeed. We're looking for funds that are based on solid financial research and follow strategies that make sense to us.

Most investors don't know this, but most of the money that goes into index funds and ETFs ends up being managed around the basis of the S&P 500 Index. That index, maintained by credit-rating giant Standard & Poor's, isn't designed to help investors. It's designed to help sell S&P's bond ratings to issuers – i.e. large public companies.

The index is "weighted" toward the stocks with the largest market caps. Funds copying this index put most of their capital into the largest and most expensive stocks. That just doesn't make sense. They are literally deciding to "buy high" instead of trying to find smart ways to "buy low." Also, there's little indication of the overall quality of the business. Bigger isn't necessarily better.

Let's jump in...

No. 1: Cambria Shareholder Yield Fund (SYLD)

The basic idea here is simple... instead of buying the entire S&P 500, our friend, fund manager Meb Faber, has organized an ETF that owns nearly equal stakes in the top 100 highest "shareholder yield" stocks in the U.S.

The list is determined by looking at the market cap (the value of all outstanding shares) and the combined value of the capital the company has returned to shareholders through dividends and share buybacks.

Over time, this keeps investors' capital in the stocks that are treating their shareholders best and that are fairly priced. The result? Nearly guaranteed outperformance of the S&P 500 without lifting a finger.

Cambria Shareholder Yield Fund (SYLD) vs. S&P 500

www.stansberryresearch.com

No. 2: WisdomTree Emerging Markets Equity Fund (DEM)

The approach here is similar to Meb's SYLD. But instead of investing in large-cap U.S. stocks that treat shareholders well, DEM owns the top 100 highest-yielding emerging-market stocks. Its top holding in mid-2014? Russia's huge natural gas company Gazprom (5.6% of the portfolio).

Investing in emerging markets is hard because of the huge volatility, the poor disclosure, and the difficulty transacting in foreign markets. On the other hand, over most market cycles, emerging markets vastly outperform U.S. stocks.

This fund allows you to own a huge basket of only the best emerging-market stocks. And it pays a large dividend to reward you while you wait out the volatility. Companies in the index are weighted based on actual cash dividends paid.

No. 3: U.S. Commodity Index Fund (USCI)

You've got to be very careful when you buy a commodity fund, like the U.S. Oil Fund (USO) or the U.S. Natural Gas Fund (UNG). These ETFs sometimes do a terrible job of converting gains in commodity prices to profits for investors. That's because they invest in futures contracts on their specific commodity. So they have to roll their futures contracts forward.

These markets are often in "contango" – meaning that the forward months' prices are much higher. In these situations, the cost of rolling their contracts forward eats up all (or most) of the profits.

The U.S. Commodity Index Fund (USCI) overcomes that problem by investing in a range of different commodities – and only when their forward-pricing curves are in "backwardation." That's the opposite of contango, and it allows the fund to make easy profits, even when commodity prices are flat.

The fund invests the other half of its assets in commodities whose prices are moving higher at a rapid pace. By hopping on some of these trends, the fund can still make money (most of the time) despite the contango.

There are a lot of moving parts here, as you can see. So for a full overview, I encourage you to read Steve's June 17, 2014 essay in our free e-letter *DailyWealth* where he published a full write-up on this unique commodity ETF.

No. 4: Blackstone Mortgage Trust (BXMT)

OK, this one is not really an ETF... It's a mortgage real estate investment trust (REIT), meaning it's a business that invests in mortgages. But it might as well be an ETF...

It's managed by Blackstone, whose real-estate head (Jonathan Gray) is the most impressive Wall Street executive I've ever met.

This is a leveraged fund that invests only in top-shelf commercial properties by owning their mortgages. It does so in a unique way that eliminates the big risks faced by most leveraged mortgage REITs.

Unlike residential real estate, commercial property has little pre-payment risk. So the fund is able to lock in its interest-rate spread by using both floating-rate financing and floating-rate mortgages. I've written about BXMT in the *Digest* before. The fund yields more than 6%.

No. 5: Market Vectors Unconventional Oil & Gas Fund (FRAK)

Simple story here: The ongoing shale boom in the U.S. is going to get bigger – far bigger than anyone realizes, even now. We've recommended our favorites in our newsletters. But one ETF gives you immediate exposure to all of the leading shale drilling firms – FRAK.

Its top 10 holdings include most of our favorites: Anadarko, EOG, Devon, Pioneer, Noble, and Chesapeake. Careful... this will surely be a volatile ETF as it is focused on a booming sector that's dependent on higher oil prices. Nevertheless, we think this is one of the best bets in the global markets right now.

No. 6: PowerShares International Dividend Achievers (PID)

This ETF owns 100 of the highest-yielding international stocks that have shares listed on one of the major global exchanges. It weights its fund into the highest-yielding stocks. (Two of its largest positions currently are units of Teekay Shipping, a company whose LNG shipping business has been a long favorite of my *Investment Advisory* newsletter).

By sticking with only companies paying a good dividend and trading on major exchanges, a lot of the risk of buying foreign stocks has been removed. Also, by holding 100 companies, it offers plenty of diversification. The weighting toward higher dividends should help produce index-beating results over time.

Lately, of course, this ETF has underperformed the U.S.-centric S&P 500... which might indicate it's a good time to buy. Certainly, this looks like a cheap index fund: The average price-to-earnings (P/E) ratio here is only 13 times earnings. And the average price-to- cash-flow ratio is a stunningly low 7 times.

No. 7: SPDR Dow Jones International Real Estate (RWX)

There's no really great international real estate ETF... yet. So in the meantime, I'd recommend just getting the broadest possible exposure to the best managers. RWX fits the bill.

Here, you're getting 100 of the biggest and best real estate firms in the world – Japan's Mitsui Fudosan, Canada's Brookfield Asset Management, Hong Kong's Link REIT, and the British Land Co. These are all legendary real estate firms... and you're getting all of them, from around the world.

Over the past five years, the returns have been good: 15% annually. Of course, that's the rebound from the global real estate crisis. But even so, I suspect the returns here will continue to be double-digit or better over the next 10 years at least.

What you have here – with just six ETFs and one U.S.-based REIT – is a group of funds that offer you value, diversification, and smart investing strategies.

What you'll pay for these funds is next to nothing. You don't need a broker. You don't need an asset planner. You don't even need to read our newsletters (although we hope you'll continue to do so anyway).

Put equal parts of your portfolio into these seven investment vehicles, and you'll rarely have a down quarter. Year after year, you'll beat the international stock indexes. And in almost every year, you'll beat the S&P 500.

Try to learn to allocate additional capital to this plan when other investors are panicking. But either way, learn to save something regularly – every month or every quarter at least.

My advice? Just allocate funds to whichever has performed the worst over the previous three years. If you do this for 15-20 years, I have no doubt you will end up with far more money than you ever dreamed was possible. If you do this for 30-40 years (you've got to start early), you'll end up stupendously wealthy.

There's no real trick to investing if you're disciplined enough to save and if you only buy good assets and good companies at reasonable prices. These funds enable you to do that, and do it well, in what I consider to be all of the major areas of equity finance: U.S. stocks, foreign stocks, emerging-market stocks, U.S. real estate, global real estate, commodities, and energy.

What's really missing in this list is the fixed-income component. I'm not recommending any fixed-income funds, as I consider bonds (both sovereign and corporate) to be in the middle of a huge bubble in 2015. What should you do for income? We'll work on that later in this series.

Speaking of the bubble in fixed-income vehicles... The U.S. Federal Reserve is afraid of what's going to happen to certain leveraged bond funds and other bond ETFs and mutual funds when interest rates rise (as we know they will, eventually).

Currently, bond-fund investors can withdraw their money on demand. But... just because the investors want out doesn't mean that there will be buyers (liquidity) in the market at that time. The result could be a catastrophe as bond funds show net asset values that bear no connection with reality.

Imagine that your bond fund says it's worth $30 a share, for example... but the bids on all of its portfolio holdings would only add up to, say, $25 a share. Who will take the $5 loss across $10 trillion of corporate bonds?

The answer is a hot potato. We could hear the chorus of "not me"s from hundreds of miles away. Jeremy Stein, a former Fed governor, put it this way: "It may be the essence of what shadow banking is... giving people a liquid claim on illiquid assets."

U.S. retail investors have placed more than $1 trillion into bond funds since early 2009. At the same time, broker/dealer bond inventory has fallen sharply. According to New York Fed data, bond-dealer inventories have fallen from $235 billion in 2007 to approximately $60 billion today.

When the bond market finally rolls over, it will cause the greatest disaster in the history of finance. Think end-of-the-Roman-Empire bad. The Fed thinks some kind of fee is going to staunch the tide? No way. All we can say is that you've been warned... both by us (hundreds of times) and now by the Federal Reserve.

Chapter 2

The Only Investments I Hope My Kids Ever Make

If you were going to limit all of your investments to only one sector of the economy – only one type of business or one kind of stock – what would you buy?

We've come to believe that for outside and passive investors (common shareholders), there are really only three sectors that offer truly extraordinary rates of return and that don't require taking any material risk. Let me be clear about what I mean...

There are three sectors of the economy where companies can establish and maintain a truly lasting competitive advantage and outside investors can identify attractive values.

As I teach my children about investing, I will focus almost entirely on examples from these three sectors. And truly... I will spend most of my time explaining only one business to my children. If they come to understand this business thoroughly, I know, with a reasonable amount of saving discipline, they will be financially secure by the time they are 30 years old... and wealthy long before they reach 50.

As part of my nine-day *Digest* series, I'm going to spend a full day explaining what we see in these sectors of the stock market. I want to show you why the investment returns are so incredibly good over the long term. I want you to know how to think about these businesses... how they work... and know a few simple keys to making great investments in these sectors.

I promise... this is all far easier than you're imagining right now. Let's start with a chart.

What Kind of a Business Always Beats the Market?

www.stansberryresearch.com

This chart shows four of the best-managed insurance companies in the United States. Company No. 1 got its start insuring contact lenses and now it mostly insures things that other companies won't touch, like oil rigs and summer camps. It's a small public company, worth about $2 billion.

Company No. 2 was founded by a Harvard graduate just out of college about 40 years ago. It is still mostly a family business (even though it has public shareholders and is worth $6 billion). It insures almost anything commercial, from yachts to elevators.

Company No. 3 is one of the world's largest insurance companies. It insures everything – homes, cars, boats, weddings (yes, weddings), etc. It is worth $33 billion.

And Company No. 4 is a major global company that (again) insures virtually anything and is worth $22 billion.

You might think, outside of being in the insurance industry, these companies have almost nothing in common. Some are small and insure essentially niche items. Others are huge, operate globally, and insure virtually anything. Yet to us, these companies look nearly the same: They are among the very best underwriters in the world.

That means these insurance companies almost always demand more in insurance premiums than they will end up spending on insurance claims. As you will soon learn, there's probably nothing more valuable in the financial world than having the skill and the discipline to underwrite insurance profitably.

Over the long term, all of these companies have generated returns that are more than double the S&P 500. They did so without taking any risk – something I'll explain more fully below. And here's the best part... their success was both inevitable and repeatable. These are not "lucky guesses" or fad-driven product sales.

One of our overriding goals at Stansberry Research is to give you the knowledge we'd want to have if our roles were reversed. Knowing what I know now about finance, I wouldn't have gotten into the investment newsletter business. I would have gotten into insurance.

There is nothing more valuable we can teach you than understanding how to invest in good insurance companies. And with the legwork we do for you in our Insurance Value Monitor (a part of our *Stansberry Data* service), it's as easy as pointing and clicking.

If a company passes our tests and you can buy it at the right price... you can be next to 100% sure that the investment will produce outstanding returns. It's like painting by numbers. Only it will make you rich.

Let me say it one more time... I believe if individuals would limit themselves to only investing in insurance companies – and no other sector – they would greatly increase their average annual returns. We don't believe that's true of any other sector of the market.

There's a simple reason for this. If you'll think about it for a minute, it should become intuitive. Here's why insurance is the world's best business: Insurance is the only business in the world that enjoys a positive cost of capital.

In every other business, companies must pay for capital. They borrow through loans. They raise equity (and must pay dividends). They pay depositors. Everywhere else you look, in every other sector, in every other type of business, the cost of capital is one of the primary business considerations. Often, it's the dominant consideration. But a well-run insurance company will routinely not only get all the capital it needs for free, it will actually be paid to accept it.

I want to make sure you understand this point. All of the people who make their living providing financial services – banks, brokers, hedge-fund managers, etc. – pay for the capital they use to earn a living. Banks borrow from depositors, investors who buy CDs, and other banks. They have to pay interest for that capital. Likewise, virtually every actor in the financial-services food chain must pay for the right to use capital. Everyone, that is, except insurance companies.

Now just follow me here for a second... Insurance companies take the premiums they've collected and they invest that capital in a range of financial assets. Assume, just for the sake of argument, that they earn 10% each year on their premiums. (That is, they make 10% on their underwriting.) And assume they invest only in the S&P 500...

What do you think the average return on their assets will be each year? In this hypothetical example, their return would be 10% plus whatever the S&P 500 returned.

In reality, of course, few insurance companies can make such a large underwriting return. And few insurance companies invest a large percentage of their portfolio in stocks. Most stick to fixed income to make sure they can always pay claims. But the point remains valid. By compounding underwriting profits over time, year after year, into the financial markets, insurance companies can produce high returns.

And here's the best part: Insurance companies don't really own most of the money they're investing. They invest the "float" they hold on behalf of their policyholders. (Float is the money they've received in premiums, but haven't paid out yet.) Underwritten appropriately, this is a risk-free way to leverage their investments and can result in astronomical returns on equity over time.

Just look at insurance company No. 1 in the previous chart. It has produced eight times the S&P 500's long-term return. Can you think of any investor, anywhere, who has done anything like that? There isn't one.

That kind of performance was only possible because, using a small equity base, the firm has invested very profitably underwritten float into solid investments, year after year.

Do you like paying taxes? Well, you won't like insurance stocks, then. They have huge tax advantages. Insurance is far and away the most tax-privileged industry in the world. Many of their investment products are totally protected from taxes. And their earnings are sheltered, too.

Insurance companies don't have to pay taxes on the cash flow they receive through premiums because, on paper, they haven't technically earned any of that money. It's not until all of the possible claims on the capital have expired that the money is "earned."

So unlike most companies that have to pay taxes on revenue and profits before investing capital, insurance companies get to invest all of the money first. This is a stupendous advantage. It's like being able to invest all the money in your paycheck – without any taxes coming out – and then paying your tax bill 10 years from now.

I realize that I can't make you (or anyone else) actually invest in insurance stocks. And I know that no matter what I say, most of you – probably more than 90% – never will. It's a tough industry to understand, filled with financial concepts and tons of jargon. But there are two reasons the smartest guys in finance wind up in insurance, one way or another...

First, it pays the best. And **second, it takes real genius to understand**. But... my goal is to make it so easy to understand and follow that any reasonably diligent reader can do so. I'd urge you to read the March 2012 issue of my *Investment Advisory* newsletter for more details about how we analyze insurance stocks.

In the meantime, I want to simply show you the one number you've got to know to invest safely and successfully.

Normal measures of valuation don't apply to insurance companies. Why not? Because regular accounting considers the "float" an insurance company holds as a liability. And technically, of course, it is.

Sooner or later, most (but not all) of that float will go out the door to cover claims. But because more premiums are always coming in the door, float tends to grow over time, not shrink. So in this way, in real life, float can be an important asset – by far the most valuable thing an insurance company owns. But there's one import- ant catch...

Float is only valuable if the company can produce an underwriting profit. If it can't, float can turn into a very expensive liability.

That's why the ability to consistently underwrite at a profit is the key – the whole key – to understanding what insurance stocks to own. Outside of underwriting discipline, almost nothing differentiates insurance companies. And they have no other way to gain a competitive advantage.

Warren Buffett – who built his fortune at Berkshire Hathaway largely on the back of profitable insurance companies – explained this in his 1977 shareholder letter:

> Insurance companies offer standardized policies, which can be copied by anyone. Their only products are promises. It is not difficult to be licensed, and rates are an open book. There are no important advantages from trademarks, patents, location, corporate longevity, raw material sources, etc., and very little consumer differentiation to produce insulation from competition.

Thus, the basis of competition between insurance companies is underwriting. That is... to be successful, insurance companies must develop the ability to accurately forecast and price risk. And they must maintain their underwriting discipline even during "soft" periods in the insurance market when premiums fall.

In our Insurance Value Monitor, we track nearly every major property and casualty insurance company in the U.S. and in Bermuda (where many operate to avoid U.S. corporate taxes completely). We rank every firm by long-term underwriting discipline. We've done the legwork for you. All you have to do is know what price to pay.

So if normal accounting doesn't apply for insurance stocks, how do you value them? Again, we went to the master, Warren Buffett, to see what he was willing to pay for very well-run insurance companies.

Bryan Beach, our lead insurance analyst, found data on three of Buffett's biggest insurance purchases. In 1998, he bought General Re for $21 billion, which added $15.2 billion to Berkshire's float and $8 billion in additional book value. So Buffett paid $0.94 for every dollar of float and book value.

Before that, in 1995, Buffett bought 49% of GEICO for $2.3 billion, which added $3 billion to Berkshire's float and $750 million in additional book value. So Buffett paid $0.61 for every dollar of float and book value.

And way back in 1967, Buffett paid $9 million for $17 million worth of National Indemnity float. That's $0.51 for every dollar of float. Looking at these numbers, we expect to pay something between $0.75 and $1 for every dollar of float and book value.

In short, there are two fundamental rules to investing in insurance stocks. Rule No. 1: Make sure the company earns an underwriting profit almost every year, no exceptions. And Rule No. 2: Never pay more than 75% of book value plus float.

Most investors will never be able to make these investments because they don't understand why underwriting discipline is so critical. And they have no ability to accurately calculate float.

Again, we've done all the hard work for you in our Insurance Value Moni-tor that's a part of our *Stansberry Data* service. We update the information monthly, and it's available for free to our Alliance members and certain groups of *Stansberry's Investment Advisory* subscribers.

If you're interested, please give our customer service staff a call at 888-261-2693. Doing so could realistically make you rich.

Chapter 3

A Sector That's Even Better Than Insurance

Pro baseball Hall-of-Famer Ted Williams didn't bat .406 in 1941 by swinging at every pitch. He carefully broke the strike zone down and decided to only swing at pitches that were in his favorite spots – his own personal strike zone.

He knew he had a much better chance of hitting those pitches than the pitchers had of throwing it into the few places where he wouldn't swing. Ted Williams only struck out 27 times that season.

The more time I spend in the financial markets, the more convinced I become that most investors should only buy stocks in these few "sweet spots." In these areas, outside investors have the tools to decide whether or not a stock is in the strike zone.

If you can learn to limit yourself to only making capital commitments in these areas – your personal "strike zone" – I'm certain you can vastly improve your results.

In the previous chapter, for example, I showed you why specific types of insurance companies (those with disciplined underwriting) almost always outperform the market.

In this chapter, I'm going to show you why, as good as insurance stocks can be, they're not where you'll find the best long-term results.

No, for the very best long-term results, you should focus on what I call capital-efficient stocks. And lucky for outside passive investors, there's one sector of the stock market that's both easy to understand and crowded with capital-efficient companies. Once you know the trick to identifying them, making a fortune in stocks is as easy as painting by numbers. Let me show you how.

Simple question: Do you think you could name any of the 20 best-performing stocks in the S&P 500 in the 50 years between 1957 and 2007? Wharton economist Jeremy Siegel wanted to answer this question thoroughly.

It's not as easy to figure out as you might think, because the composition of the S&P 500 changes frequently. Siegel had to go back and get the actual list of stocks from 1957 and then follow each one, carefully, to see how much it paid out in dividends, spinoffs, mergers, and liquidations.

So... what were the real best-performing stocks over that 50-year period?

Company	Return
Philip Morris	19.8%
Abbott Labs	16.5%
Bristol-Myers	16.4%
Tootsie Roll	16.1%
Pfizer	16.0%
Coca-Cola	16.0%
Merck	15.9%
PepsiCo	15.5%
Colgate-Palmolive	15.2%
Crane	15.1%
H.J. Heinz	14.8%
Wrigley	14.7%
Fortune Brands	14.6%
Kroger	14.4%
Schering-Plough	14.4%
Procter & Gamble	14.3%
Hershey Foods	14.2%
Wyeth	14.0%
Royal Dutch Pet.	13.6%
General Mills	13.6%
Source: Jeremy Siegel, The Future For Investors	

What I'm sure you can see for yourself is that, almost without exception, these companies sell high-margin products (some are extremely high-margin), in stable industries that are dominated by a handful of well-known brand names.

Look at the top 10 names on the list – the ones that produced 15%-plus annual returns. My bet is that most of you have at least three or four of these companies' products in your house at all times. (Crane, by the way, is the obvious exception.)

What is it that Crane (a maker of high-margin industrial parts) has in common with these other companies? It's extraordinarily capital-efficient.

Because of Crane's excellent, storied reputation (it has been in business since 1855)... the unique, proprietary nature of its products... and the stable, long-term nature of its business, Crane doesn't have to spend a fortune on brand advertising or building new manufacturing plants to come up with new products every few years.

This means that as sales grow, the amount of capital that must be reinvested in the business doesn't grow much – or at all. Over the last 10 years, Crane has earned gross profits of nearly $8 billion and spent just $312 million on capital investments.

I learned the basic concepts behind capital efficiency by carefully studying the few large investments Warren Buffett made in the 1970s and 1980s. If you read his 1983 letter to shareholders, he basically gives the whole strategy away. But it's hidden... at the very end of the letter... underneath the headline: "Goodwill and its Amortization: The Rules and the Realities."

You can read Buffett's letter if you'd like... but I think you'll learn more about the practical application of this strategy if you go back and re-read my December 2007 *Investment Advisory*, where I recommended shares of Hershey.

I've said many times, and in many places, that I believe my recommendation of Hershey will likely be the best stock pick I make in my entire career. I fully expect the investment to deliver 15% annual returns over the long term – the very long term.

As I said when I recommended it, "the longer you hold this stock, the more rapidly your wealth will compound and you'll never have to sell – ever."

In my initial recommendation, I noted how capital efficient Hershey is...

> Over the last 10 years, the company's annual capital spending has remained essentially unchanged. In 1997, the firm invested $172 million in additions to property and equipment. By the end of 2006, the annual capital budget had only increased to $198 million – a paltry 15%. Meanwhile, cash profits and dividends nearly doubled.
>
> This is the beauty of capital-efficient businesses: As sales and profits grow, capital investments don't. Thus, the amount of money that's available to return to shareholders not only grows in nominal dollars, it also grows as a percentage of sales. In 1999, dividends paid out equaled 3.4% of sales. But by 2006, the company spent $735 million on dividends and share buybacks, an amount equal to 14.8% of sales.

Nearly seven years later, Hershey's sales have grown to more than $7 billion, but capital investments remain incredibly small – less than 5% of sales. In 2013, with gross profits of more than $3 billion, Hershey distributed $550 million to shareholders. That's nearly 20% of gross profits and far more capital than it invested in its operations ($325 million).

That's another hallmark of capital-efficient companies: They almost always return more capital to shareholders each year than they spend in capital investments. Why doesn't Hershey distribute even more?

It could... Cash flows from operations were more than $1 billion. But companies like Hershey will wait to buy back lots of stock (or make wise acquisitions) when prices are low. How can you do the same? How do you know when is the right time to buy these stocks, which almost always trade at rich premiums to the average S&P 500 stock?

Capital Efficiency in Action

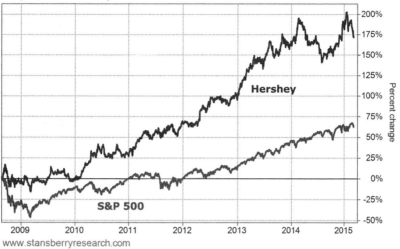

www.stansberryresearch.com

You want to buy these stocks during the rare times they're cheap enough to safely take themselves private. Again, I explained the concept in my December 2007 issue...

> Hershey's enterprise value is $11.5 billion. That's the amount of money it would require to pay off all the company's debts and buy back all the outstanding shares of stock at the current price.
>
> The company earns more than $1 billion before taxes, interest, and depreciation. Its earnings are very consistent, and its brand places it in the upper tier of all businesses around the world. It could easily finance a bond offering large enough to buy itself – or "go private."
>
> Thus, I think it is extremely unlikely that investors will lose money buying the stock at today's price... Given the company could easily finance the repurchase of all its stocks and bonds, I believe buying this stock is no more or less risky than buying its bonds.
>
> That is the true definition of a "no risk" stock – an analysis of its cash flow shows it could afford to buy back both all of its debts and all of its shares... These situations are extremely attractive because, while you're only taking a risk that's similar to a bondholder, you're getting ownership of all of the company's future earnings.

You know when it's safe to buy these businesses by figuring out if they could finance a debt issuance in excess of their enterprise value. That can be a little tricky. So use a rule of thumb. These stocks are safe to buy (and likely to produce incredible long-term results) when you can buy them for around 10 years' worth of current cash flows from operations.

There's an easy way to keep your eye out for these world-class, long-term investments. We maintain a "Capital Efficiency Monitor" as part of our supplementary *Stansberry Data* service. We do all the legwork (of course) and list the companies that are capital-efficient and whose shares are trading at a reasonable price (around 10 times cash flow).

You will also find businesses like these by looking in the portfolios of high-quality investors. I've noticed that Mario Gabelli's GAMCO team loves these kinds of businesses. Likewise, of course, the exchange-traded fund I mentioned in Chapter 1 – Meb Faber's Cambria Shareholder Yield Fund (SYLD) – is always going to feature a lot of these names, as companies have to be reasonably capital efficient and reasonably priced if they're going to rank in the top spots in terms of shareholder yield.

Here's another helpful hint when it comes to this type of investing: It's critical to avoid companies who are returning huge amounts of capital to investors simply because their businesses have become obsolete. Companies like Western Union, for example, might look good on paper, but its future cash flows are seriously in jeopardy by new technologies.

If you're going to invest using this strategy, you want to stick to the highest-quality businesses, whose products are timeless. I always ask myself this question: "Are my grandkids likely to want this brand and this product?"

There's no brand or business in the world that will last forever, but you should try to focus on the stuff that's as close to forever as possible.

Here's another valuable tip. This is one of the few, genuine secrets to investing that I've ever learned. In fact, it's a little creepy. Stansberry Research Editor in Chief Brian Hunt first pointed it out to me: **A lot of the companies that fit into our model of capital efficiency sell products that are highly addictive**. Says Hunt...

If you look at the list of the 20 best-performing S&P 500 stocks during that time frame that kept their general corporate structure intact, you'll note many of them sold habit-forming products. It jumps right out at you.

For example, Phillip Morris is at the top of the list. It was the top-performing S&P 500 stock from 1957 to 2007. It sold cigarettes, which contained addictive nicotine. Fortune Brands, which was called American Brands for a while, is on the list. It sold cigarettes and alcohol.

Coca-Cola and PepsiCo are on the list. They sold soda, which is a sugar-delivery vehicle. Hershey Foods and Tootsie Roll are on the list. They sold chocolate and sugar. Wrigley is on the list. It sold sugary gum, like Big Red and Juicy Fruit. People love to get a little sugar rush. It's habit-forming.

Many drug companies are also on the list. These names include Abbott Labs, Bristol-Myers Squibb, Merck, Wyeth, Schering-Plough, and Pfizer. People get very, very accustomed to taking certain drugs. Much of the time, those drugs are useful, although sometimes they are not. I'm not saying they are good or bad, I'm simply pointing out that people get very accustomed – even addicted – to taking them.

You can make the case that some fast foods are addictive as well. Fast food is loaded with fat and sugar – stuff that makes people crave it. This is part of the reason McDonald's has been such a corporate success. McDonald's has returned an average of 13% a year for three decades, making investors extremely rich.

And the reason why it did so well is simple. When people form a habit around a product, it goes a long way toward ensuring repeat business. People get used to brands, and they grow resistant to switching. Also, when people get used to a product and the brand surrounding it, they are more likely to continue buying the product, even if the price increases a little.

Both of these help companies sustain sales growth and healthy profit margins. That's good for shareholders. It's also important to know that when these companies hit upon the right recipes or the right mix of whatever it takes to make good products, they don't have to make large, ongoing investments in the business. They don't have to spend tons of money on further research and development. Once Coca-Cola hit upon Coke, it didn't have to change it. The same goes for Budweiser, Hershey, and Tootsie Roll.

When you develop a product that people love and develop habits around, you don't tinker with it. You don't have to spend a lot of money on new research and development. You don't have to buy expensive, high-tech equipment. This means a larger percentage of revenues can be sent to shareholders – it's a capital-efficient business.

One more thing... I don't expect all (or even most) of the market's leaders from 1957 to 2007 to remain at the top of the performance charts. But what I hope you'll notice is that the characteristics of the leading companies are the same. New brands come along and make small changes... and get very popular. New medicines are invented. New forms of addiction are marketed successfully.

If you keep your eyes open, it's not all that hard to figure out which of these products and businesses are likely to do extremely well over the long term. On the next page, you'll find the list of the 10 best-performing stocks in the S&P 500 over the last 20 years (on an annualized basis):

Company	Return
Biogen	37.9%
Keurig	37.0%
Monster Beverage	36.9%
Gilead	33.3%
Celgene	32.6%
KC Southern	26.9%
Apple	25.7%
Ross	24.3%
Express Scripts	24.2%
Qualcomm	24.0%
Time Warner	23.4%
Regeneron	21.7%
Precision Cast	21.0%
O'Reilly Auto	20.7%
Autonation	20.5%
Tractor Supply	20.5%
Starbucks	20.4%
TJX	20.0%
Expeditors International	19.9%

The top five firms sell high-margin, branded drugs – as long as you agree that caffeine is a highly addictive drug. Likewise, although most people don't think about Starbucks as being a drug company, its decaf coffee contains more caffeine than McDonald's regular coffee does.

What is it really selling? Over the last 10 years, Starbucks has produced gross profits of $57 billion. It has only spent $7.3 billion on capital investments. It spent $5.5 billion buying back stock and another $1.7 billion on cash dividends.

In short, even though it had to pay for a huge international build out, it has still been able to spend almost as much on its shareholders as it did on growing its business. That's pretty remarkable and an excellent indication that long-term shareholders in Starbucks will do very well...

Selling Addictive Drugs Is a Great Business

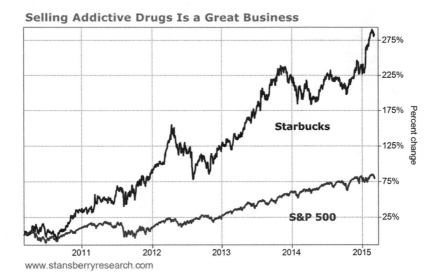

www.stansberryresearch.com

— Chapter 4 —

How to Make Commodity Investing Risk-Free

Resources undoubtedly seem like an unusual and risky investment choice. But in this chapter, we'll discuss a slight twist that hopefully will make sense to you. **It's a way of understanding commodities that actually makes them risk-free**.

First, though... congratulations are in order. When we decided to get "long" natural gas following that commodity's bottom in the spring of 2012, I asked *Stansberry's Investment Advisory* analyst and longtime friend David Lashmet to go to Texas and learn all that he could, on the ground, about the prospects for exporting our country's massive energy bounty.

He spent months on this project. He came back with one word: propane. It was a brilliant discovery. You see, although it's essentially against the law to export crude oil – and although it will take another five years or so before liquefied natural gas (LNG) facilities that are being built now will be able to export a significant amount of methane (aka natural gas) – there were facilities and boats available to export propane.

And as the price of propane plummeted because of soaring domestic supplies, one company moved aggressively to buy up and control most of the available export capacity in the U.S. As Dave discovered, that company was Targa Resources (TRGP).

This was one of the greatest investment opportunities I had seen in my entire career. As we explained in the December 2012 issue of my *Investment Advisory*...

> Thanks to government tariffs, regulations, and licenses, it's almost impossible to get the huge new supplies of domestic energy out of the U.S. The one exception is the clean-burning, easily stored NGL family of fuels – mostly propane. And Targa controls one of the

country's two propane export terminals, as well as the entire associated infra- structure necessary to supply it. Besides Cheniere, that's as close to an American export monopoly as you're going to get.

At the time of our purchase, Targa was a newly created company that had been created by private-equity firm Warburg Pincus. The company's primary initial assets were purchased from failed energy-trading firm Dynegy. At the time we wrote about the business, few people had ever heard of Targa, even in Texas.

David did a fantastic job of following the energy surplus, literally down the pipes, to figure out who would be able to gain the huge profits available to companies that could acquire energy supplies at U.S. prices and sell them at foreign prices. It was Targa that owned that "bridge."

By figuring this out, David helped our subscribers earn tremendous profits. The stock marched straight up...

Massive Profits Exporting U.S. Energy Supplies

Targa Resources has soared higher (3½-year chart)

www.stansberryresearch.com

We first recommended the stock below $60 a share. Yesterday, the stock rose 25% to close at $150. My subscribers are up 218% in 18 months. (Porter note: Since this essay was written, Targa's share price has fallen.)

That's great, of course, and we congratulate Dave on this result. But... what matters even more to me than the stupendous profits is that Dave nailed the "why." He didn't just deliver big gains – which often enough happens randomly. He delivered the critical piece of information that allowed us to profit on a huge and important trend in our economy. How do I know?

Yesterday, Targa's price soared because of a $15 billion offer to acquire the company. The bidder? Energy Transfer Partners (ETE). Dave recommended that company, too – about a year after he recommended Targa. And we're up a huge 67% on ETE in just 10 months.

Dave's work here is stunning – by far the best energy analysis I've seen anywhere over the last two years... and by a wide margin. When there's an important, valuable, and complicated opportunity to pursue, I send Dave.

Now, let's get back to how we think about investing in commodities... and how, if done correctly, commodity investments can be almost risk-free. Rather than give you a bunch of theory, I'd rather show you precisely how I put these ideas to work, starting in 2012.

I was a vehement and frequent critic of "Peak Oil." Promoters of this idea were the most intellectually dishonest people I have ever met. The true believers were worse. They were criminally stupid. There was no way we were going to run out of oil or any other hydrocarbon. Not any time in the next 100 or more years.

But such arguments did scare people. They sold a lot of books. They raised a lot of money for oil companies, even for idiots who proposed importing natural gas into the American market. (That's like setting up a business to import oil to Saudi Arabia.)

Meanwhile, while the press and the promoters were crowing about Peak Oil and starting a panic, the actual leaders of the oil business in the United States were figuring out how to combine hydraulic fracking and horizontal drilling to produce huge amounts of gas and oil from shale rock.

One of the first was Mitchell Energy, which began producing huge volumes of gas out of the Barnett Shale (north of Dallas) in the early 2000s.

Devon bought the company for $3.5 billion in 2001. Note the date. By 2001, everyone in the oil business knew very well that large increases to domestic onshore production were possible. It took a while, of course, for the industry to figure how to optimize and economize the strategies that Mitchell pioneered. Those efforts, in fact, continue today.

But everyone should have known, as I did, that new technology, massive increases to drilling, and rapidly growing production would eventually create a glut. The risk wasn't that we would run out of hydrocarbon. The risk was that too much capital would be invested in the fields and that a glut would develop.

As early as 2006, I began to warn that a huge natural gas glut was inevitable. From the June 2006 issue of my *Investment Advisory*...

> As more rigs come online and consumers use less natural gas because of its high price, guess what is bound to happen? A glut of natural gas, with more and more natural gas in storage. Is that happening? Is there a glut of natural gas developing? Right now, there's 41% more natural gas in storage than average for this time of year.
>
> That's how markets work: the price of the commodity goes up, increased production follows, consumer behavior is impacted by higher prices, and, eventually, a surplus leads to lower prices.
>
> It's not about Peak Oil. It's simply a regular commodity cycle. Boom precedes bust. And when it comes to natural gas, unlike housing, we can't just sit on the extra capacity. It has to be either stored or liquidated. That's why natural gas prices might go lower than anyone expects, for a long time... Natural gas could fall even further to below $3.

Keep in mind, when I wrote that, I had no idea that the global economy would collapse in 2008. I simply knew that there was far too much capital being put to work in oil and gas fields... that prices were far too high based on inventories... and that marginal producers would continue producing for years, simply to keep cash coming in the door.

In fact, as late as 2009, I was still expecting natural gas to fall below $3 per thousand cubic feet (MCF). At a conference that March, I famously told global resource expert and longtime natural gas investor Rick Rule, "If you're long natural gas, you should have your head examined." I then bet him a case of fine Bordeaux that prices would continue falling, to below $3. They did. (Rick, being a man of his word, paid up.)

I want you to understand... I wasn't trying to predict the future. I simply knew that all over the U.S., formerly marginal drilling sites were being turned into gushers with new technology that was becoming more and more efficient. I knew that production was soaring. And I knew that natural gas consumption was falling because high prices were leading power companies to burn more coal.

Supply was soaring. Demand was falling. Inventories were bulging. And best of all, the public was fully entranced by the nonsense of Peak Oil. There was only one possible outcome: a huge glut of natural gas. This isn't rocket science. It's common sense. You can see what inevitably happened in this next chart...

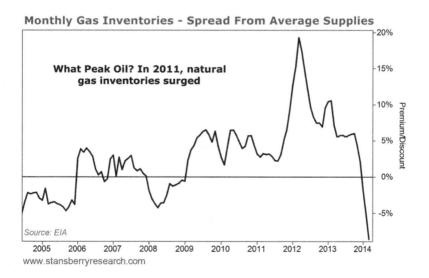

Monthly Gas Inventories - Spread From Average Supplies

What Peak Oil? In 2011, natural gas inventories surged

Source: EIA

www.stansberryresearch.com

The trick to buying commodities is to wait until there's a bust. Wait until prices for the commodity have fallen so low that producers can't produce the commodity at a profit. Wait until inventories have surged and rolled over. Wait until prices have reached a nonsensical level. And remember... these trends take a long time to develop.

With natural gas, I went from bearish to bullish in the spring of 2012. Here's what I wrote in my April 2012 issue, titled "The Best Opportunities of the Next Two Years"...

> I am extremely bullish on natural gas... For most investors, the opportunity unfolding in natural gas will be one of the best investment opportunities of the next decade. Right now, natural gas is so cheap, many companies are simply flaring it off – burning it – rather than bothering to pipe it across the country and sell it. Not only that, but right now you can buy natural gas reserves in the stock market for free.
>
> Sooner or later, the price of natural gas will rebound sharply... and not just because it always has in the past. What will propel natural gas prices over the medium term (say, five years) is an economic truism: It's impossible for a surplus of energy to exist for long.
>
> As prices fall, more and more uses for natural gas will appear. At some price, natural gas becomes competitive with other forms of energy. You ought to buy all the natural gas you can afford because these energy resources will not be cheap forever.

By the spring of 2012, I knew a few things that gave me total confidence that natural gas prices had reached a bottom. First, I knew that at the current spot price (less than $2 per MCF), it was impossible for any of the independent natural gas companies (Devon, Chesapeake, Anadarko, Southwestern, Encana, WPX, and Ultra) to make money.

The next chart shows how their operating margins were collapsing as their hedges rolled off and they began transacting at the new, much lower price of gas...

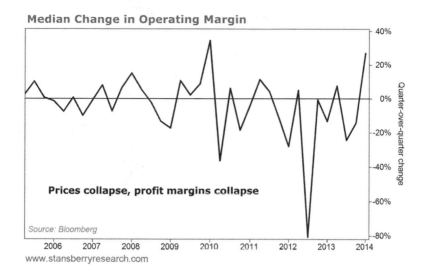

Median Change in Operating Margin

Prices collapse, profit margins collapse

Source: Bloomberg

www.stansberryresearch.com

Next, because natural gas is only one form of hydrocarbon energy, I could see that it had reached a comparative price that was simply unthinkable. The real commodity you're buying when you buy natural gas is energy. At some price, all forms of hydrocarbons are relatively interchangeable. For example, right now there's a plant being built in Louisiana to refine natural gas into gasoline.

That's because, compared with oil, natural gas is still far too cheap on an energy-equivalent basis. For decades, oil has been about 10 times more expensive than natural gas, on average, on an energy-equivalent basis.

But by the spring of 2012, oil was trading at price equal to more than 50 times the price of natural gas. There was no way that such a price disparity would last, because one form of energy is ultimately interchangeable with another...

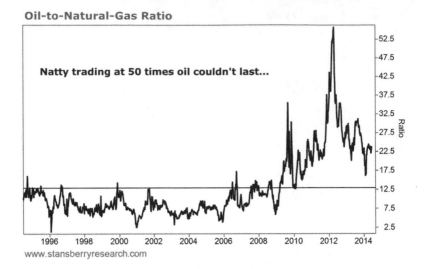

Oil-to-Natural-Gas Ratio

Natty trading at 50 times oil couldn't last...

All right... by the spring of 2012, we could see that a glut had developed (as we had expected). We could see that prices had collapsed to historic lows. We could see that the marginal producers (the U.S. independents) were going to experience massive operating losses.

But how did we know the time was truly right? Our timing was dictated by significant reductions to both production and inventories.

This next chart shows the natural gas rig count maintained by oil-services giant Baker Hughes. It's the number of rigs currently working in the U.S. to produce natural gas. You can see that in 2012, the rig count plummeted. That's the producers "taking their ball and going home."

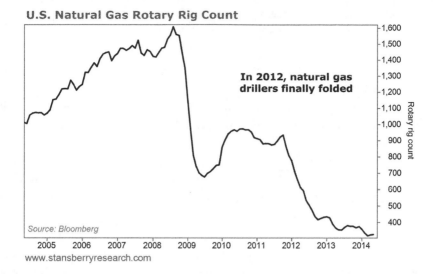

U.S. Natural Gas Rotary Rig Count

In 2012, natural gas drillers finally folded

Rotary rig count

Source: Bloomberg

2005 2006 2007 2008 2009 2010 2011 2012 2013 2014

www.stansberryresearch.com

This move – plus a large and surprising decline in natural gas inventories in March 2012 – was the final sign I had been waiting to see. The neat thing about commodity markets is that they are purely logical. High prices (during a boom) spur production and cause consumers to cut back consumption.

But at the bottom, the opposite occurs. Over the last two years, we saw all kinds of new demand for natural gas emerge because the price has been low. We've seen a surge in exports (see the Targa story earlier). We've seen power companies switching from coal back to natural gas. And we've seen global manufacturing relocate to the U.S. to take advantage of the surplus of cheap energy – particularly the petrochemical industry.

If you go back and look at the best-performing S&P 500 companies over the long term, you'll find that almost all the companies are either capital efficient (mostly drug companies and companies with addictive products) or energy companies. That's because the operating margins and returns on investment in the resource sector (particularly energy) can be huge.

Investing in commodity stocks is generally perceived as risky. But using a small amount of common sense and information that's widely available to all investors, it's not only possible, but it's easy to identify safe opportunities to invest in commodities. The trick is waiting until prices are so low that the entire production industry is failing and then not 'pulling the trigger' until inventories begin to sharply decline.

The other trick is remembering that these cycles are long-lived. You might only get the kind of opportunity we saw in natural gas back in 2012 once or twice every 20 years. You have to watch these markets over the long term and be prepared to make large commitments when the time is right.

There are two more things you should know about investing in commodities... two genuine "inside" secrets that few people will ever explain to you. If you watch the cycle develop like I describe above, you can reduce your risk by 90%. All you have to be is patient.

You can't force a commodity price cycle to change. If you're able to be patient, you can virtually eliminate the remaining risk by only investing in royalty-paying securities. These are companies – like natural gas royalty trust San Juan Royalty Trust (SJT) – that simply own royalty interests in wells or mines.

The cool thing about these trusts is that their payout increases tend to follow commodity-price changes by about six months. If you look at San Juan Royalty Trust, for example, it really began to move higher in 2013, even though natural gas prices bottomed in April 2012. We call this the "royal" delay. It gives investors a second chance to buy into the bottom of a commodity.

That's great for obvious reasons, but the real reason royalty trusts help you eliminate investment risk is because they don't have any debt or any overhead. It's next to impossible for them to go bankrupt.

The "Royal" Delay

Royalty stocks often trail commodity prices by six to 12 months, offering investors a "second chance" to invest at the bottom... (5-year chart)

Price per share

www.stansberryresearch.com

The other, safer option than buying the producers is to focus on the "picks and shovels" companies. Take Halliburton, for example. It's the leading provider of services to the production companies I listed earlier.

Its shares are up 150% over the last two years! That's a far better return than almost all producers' shares.

The great thing about buying a well-run service company is that you get industry-wide diversification, as all production companies use Halliburton's services. Thus, you don't have to try and figure out which fields are the best or which producer is going to strike the biggest wells.

Whoever is doing best, they will be using Halliburton. You can accomplish much the same by buying ETFs that hold stakes in all of the producers, like FRAK, for example.

The point is, if you're trying to invest in the commodity price cycle, it can be very low risk if you're buying securities like royalty trusts, service companies, or ETFs that don't have any single-stock risk. If you combine this approach with buying a few of the highest-quality producers (think EOG in the Eagle Ford, Devon in the Permian, or Continental in the Bakken), I'm sure you'll be successful.

The commodity price cycles I'm watching right now are coal and uranium. I think uranium has a long way to go. But coal looks very interesting...

That wraps up our review of the three best sectors for outside, passive, common shareholders to invest in. Two of my three choices are intuitive: **Insurance companies can produce consistent, market-beating returns for long periods if they're able to underwrite policies at a profit**. Buying these kinds of insurance stocks is just about the safest and best form of investing I've ever discovered.

Next, **I don't think it's difficult for any investor to identify companies that have great brands, great business models (capital efficient), and products that are addictive**. I would personally avoid drug stocks, at least as individual securities, because I've found it's near impossible to figure out which company's new drug will be accepted by the FDA, etc.

That still leaves plenty of profitable businesses. See my recent recommendation of Lorillard – it's a classic bet on capital efficiency. Keep in mind, these are long-term bets. Real outperformance in these stocks typically won't emerge for five or 10 years. You must be patient and learn to buy at the right time (ideally, when other investors panic).

Finally, **although most investors think investing in commodity businesses is very risky... I believe if you're willing to time the commodity price cycle and if you focus on royalty firms and "picks and shovels" plays, these investments can be among the safest you'll ever make**.

In the right circumstances, you can produce trades with zero downside and huge upside potential. Just remember to wait for historically low prices, collapsing profit margins (in the producers), and suddenly shrinking inventories.

— Chapter 5 —

Our Most Controversial Strategy: Beating the Market

Out of all of the things I've said or written in my career, the thing that gets me in the most "hot water" is my view that you can and should time the market.

When I write "you," I don't mean some representative sample or some investor somewhere. No, I mean you... the person reading this book... the person who is going to put his savings at risk when he invests in the stock or bond market. You.

A lot of people – even some smart ones – believe trying to time the market is a fool's errand. They argue that the best you can do is simply plow your savings, year after year, into a mutual fund or index fund. These folks make a whole range of arguments and back them up with plenty of "facts."

They'll cite academic studies and average investor results. They will say, again and again, that "no one" can beat the market, so why should anyone try?

I disagree... completely.

Let's start here. Let's say they're right. If the market is really efficient, it shouldn't matter when you invest or what you buy. If that's really the case, then why not try to do better? As long as you're investing in something, you should do alright, according to these folks. So what's the harm in trying to beat the market?

And here's another way to look at it. The efficient-market folks love to argue that it's impossible for the average investor to beat the market because it's impossible for most people to beat the average result.

At some point, it is a mathematical certainty that not everyone can beat the market. But just because something is "true" on average or across a population doesn't necessarily mean it must be true for you.

For example, I might argue on average, everyone who marries will end up with a marginally attractive spouse of normal intelligence. Therefore, you're probably wasting your time trying to find a beautiful and intelligent person to marry you. In theory, that might be good advice. But was that your dating strategy? If you had dated any dog that would have you, would you have married the spouse you wanted?

In short... when it comes to a lot of important things in our lives, getting better-than-average results is a worthy goal. Luckily for investors, I don't believe beating the market is nearly as hard as trying to date a supermodel.

I'm 100% convinced that anyone with normal intelligence and a modicum of emotional stability can do it. There are a few simple and logical reasons why...

The reasons come from Wall Street's irrational focus on short-term "earnings" and most investors' total lack of discipline. In this chapter, I'm going to give you my five keys to timing the market. If you use my strategy, I guarantee you can double your average investment results over 10 years... or maybe even do a lot better.

But listen... there's an entire army of people out there whose careers depend on you never doubting the idea that the markets are perfectly efficient and you can't beat the market. If you speak to any of these millions of people in the financial services industry about my ideas, they will tell you I'm a fool, liar, or fraud. So get ready for an argument. Listen carefully. You'll notice these folks won't ever discuss the merits of my actual strategy.

You see, the financial industry can only survive and prosper if you're willing to give it your assets to manage. The industry needs you to believe that it's always a good time to put your money in the market. And it needs you to believe that you can't do it yourself. That's why when I write things like this essay, folks in or supported by the financial industry go bananas.

As far as who is right and wrong... listen to what the oldest and wisest newsletter writer, Richard Russell, says about market timing in his classic essay, *Rich Man, Poor Man...*

In the investment world, the wealthy investor has one major advantage over the little guy, the stock market amateur and the neophyte trader. The advantage that the wealthy investor enjoys is that he doesn't need the markets... The wealthy investor doesn't need the markets because he already has all the income he needs...

The wealthy investor tends to be an expert on values. When bonds are cheap and bond yields are irresistibly high, he buys bonds. When stocks are on the bargain table and stock yields are attractive, he buys stocks.

When real estate is a great value, he buys real estate. When great art or fine jewelry or gold is on the "give away" table, he buys art or diamonds or gold. In other words, the wealthy investor puts his money where the great values are.

And if no outstanding values are available, the wealthy investor waits. He can afford to wait. He has money coming in daily, weekly, monthly. The wealthy investor knows what he is looking for, and he doesn't mind waiting months or even years for his next investment.

But what about the little guy? This fellow always feels pressured to "make money." And in return, he's always pressuring the market to "do something" for him. But sadly, the market isn't interested.

When the little guy isn't buying stocks offering 1% or 2% yields, he's off to Las Vegas or Atlantic City trying to beat the house at roulette. Or he's spending 20 bucks a week on lottery tickets, or he's "investing" in some crackpot scheme that his neighbor told him about (in strictest confidence, of course).

And because the little guy is trying to force the market to do something for him, he's a guaranteed loser. The little guy doesn't understand values, so he constantly overpays... The little guy is the typical American, and he's deeply in debt.

Now... think about what Richard Russell said. Ask yourself, do you invest like the poor man or the rich man? How much do you know about the value of what you've bought? How long did you wait for the right opportunity to buy it? What's your downside? What are you expecting as your result? In a year? In three years? In five years? In 10 years?

The poor man can't even imagine a 10-year investment return. Nothing he buys lasts that long. Of course, if you want to get rich in stocks, almost everything you buy should last that long. It's the compound returns that will make you rich, not the quick trades.

What does Warren Buffett, perhaps the greatest investor ever, say? Is the market so perfectly efficient that knowledgeable and patient investors have no opportunity to earn excess returns? Buffett argues that all the value investors he knows – those who broadly followed the tenets of Ben Graham and David Dodd, authors of the value-investing bible *Security Analysis* – have beaten the market by a wide margin.

This isn't an accident or a coin flip. These investors all used the same principles to guide their choices. Their picks were not random or lucky. They involved all different types of securities and strategies. The only common theme was an intense focus on understanding the value of each security purchased.

As Warren Buffett wrote in *The Super Investors of Graham and Doddsville*...

> The common intellectual theme of the investors from Graham-and-Doddsville is this: They search for discrepancies between the value of a business and the price of small pieces of that business in the market.
>
> I'm convinced that there is much inefficiency in the market. These Graham-and-Doddsville investors have successfully exploited gaps between price and value.
>
> When the price of a stock can be influenced by a "herd" on Wall Street with prices set at the margin by the most emotional person, or the greediest person, or the most depressed person, it is hard to argue that the market always prices rationally. In fact, market prices are frequently nonsensical.
>
> I have seen no trend toward value investing in the 35 years that I've practiced it. There seems to be some perverse human characteristic

that likes to make easy things difficult. The academic world, if anything, has actually backed away from the teaching of value investing over the last 30 years. It's likely to continue that way.

Ships will sail around the world but the Flat Earth Society will flourish. There will continue to be wide discrepancies between price and value in the marketplace, and those who read their Graham & Dodd will continue to prosper.

Step 1 in our guide to beating the market is based on the ideas of the men above. **Before you buy a stock or bond (or anything else), ask yourself, "What's the intrinsic value of what I'm buying? And how does that intrinsic value compare with what I'm going to have to pay for it?"** Always make sure you're buying at a good price.

There are lots of ways to estimate intrinsic value. And as with the value of a house, there's no one right answer. If I asked you to estimate the value of your home, you could give me a range based on similar sales in your area.

You could tell me "replacement cost" based on what a lot nearby would cost and the construction costs. You could give me the tax basis. And I could look up what the insurance company estimates your house is worth (that's usually the most accurate).

The point is, people of normal intelligence can figure out what something is really worth. When it comes to publicly traded stocks, plenty of information is available to help you do the same.

When we look at stocks, we generally assign them an intrinsic value that's based on cash flow (how much cash this company can generate) for operating companies or a "take-out" price for asset-development stocks.

In general, public companies fall into one of these two categories. They're either operating businesses (which are designed to make annual profits) or asset-development businesses (which may have many years of losses as they build out something like a gold mine, oilfield, or new drug).

Simple rules of thumb? Never pay more than about 10 times the maximum annual free cash flow for operating companies. Never pay more than half of the appraised value of an asset-development company.

The next part of our strategy to "time" the market – Step 2 – is even easier. There's not really any math involved: **Become a connoisseur of value**. Look around the world. What are other investors running away from? Is there a safe way to invest? Is it extremely cheap? Does this opportunity seem like one of the greatest deals you've ever seen?

Let me give you an extreme example. When trouble started brewing between Russia and Ukraine in early 2014, President Obama's spokesman, Jay Carney, said on March 18: "If I were you, I wouldn't invest in Russian equities right now, unless you're going short." As a connoisseur of value, this would prick your ears...

Russian energy stocks have been the cheapest, high-quality equities available anywhere in the world for several quarters. They pay big dividends. They have valuable assets. They are dirt cheap – trading for two and three times earnings and for a tiny fraction of their asset values.

Gazprom, for example, holds assets worth more than $400 billion. Today, even after the recent increase in stock price, the company's enterprise value (the value of all of its outstanding shares and its debts) is only $144 billion.

Being a Russian company means that Gazprom's stock will probably always trade at some discount. But a discount greater than 60%? And when a leading barometer of the public's thinking – the president's spokesman – makes a call about stock prices, it's almost like someone is sending you an invitation to make money.

Now, I concede... that's certainly an extreme example. But similar things happen all the time, things that don't involve as much risk as Russian equities. And if you're willing to focus on the areas of the market that offer outstanding value, you will come across opportunities like these frequently.

On the other hand, if you're only following what the folks on CNBC are talking about, you'll never see values like this one. The key is to focus on the areas of the market where value abounds. And then... to be patient and wait for the "dinner bell" to ring.

Step 3 in our guide to beating the market is even easier. **Learn to make big commitments only when other investors are clearly panicking, stocks are cheap, and extremely safe investments are available**. This is what most people mean when they say market "timing." This is what I mean when I say "allocate to value." Two quick examples...

First, in the fall of 2008, investors were clearly panicking. Warren Buffett even wrote a letter to the *New York Times* explaining why it was time to buy stocks hand over fist – and was criticized on CNBC for doing so! If there has ever been a better contrarian indicator, I've never seen it.

Meanwhile, you could have bought shares of iconic beer maker Anheuser-Busch (BUD) – a stock I first recommended in 2006 – for around $50 for several weeks in October and November. At the time, global brewer InBev had an all-cash deal in place to buy the stock for $70 per share. I told investors the situation was so safe, they should put 25% of their assets into the shares.

It was the easiest and safest way to make a lot of money I'd ever seen. Even if the deal fell through (and it couldn't; it was an all-cash deal at a reasonable price)... the stock was worth far more than $50 a share. In my view, there was zero downside, and an almost certain $15-$20 profit in just a few days.

A few months later – in February 2009 – shares of renowned jeweler Tiffany were trading for less than $25. The company has large inventories of gold and precious stones. Subtracting the value of its inventory from its debt load and dividing by the shares outstanding, gave you liquidation value of around $24 per share.

In short, you could buy Tiffany – one of the premier luxury brands in the world – for the value of its current inventory. That means, you could have gotten the real estate, the brand, and all the future profits for free.

Again, I remember the specifics of the trade because I wrote about this situation to subscribers. It's times like these when you must be willing to make large commitments.

Fine, you might say. But what should I do, just hold cash for years or decades, waiting for a perfect situation? Stocks were only as cheap as they were in 2009 three or four times over the last 100 years.

No, I don't argue that you should stay 100% in cash until stocks crash. That is probably the biggest misunderstanding most investors have about our advice. We never advocate selling everything.

We didn't sell everything in 2008, even though we knew the mortgage associations Fannie Mae and Freddie Mac were going to zero and that Wall Street was going to collapse. And we haven't recommended selling everything now, even though we have grave concerns about the stability of the global monetary system.

We never believe that we can predict the future accurately. Instead, we want to build a portfolio that will thrive over time, no matter what happens. Today, we see that stocks are no longer great values. It's harder for us to find good opportunities. And so, we've told subscribers, to begin building cash.

When you sell something, sock away the profits until better opportunities emerge. When do you sell? Well, that depends. But no matter what, follow your trailing stop losses. And that leads us to...

Step 4: Stay reasonably diversified, use trailing-stop losses, and always maintain a large cash reserve. Here we part ways with most value investors. A lot of good value investors refuse to use trailing-stop losses. Instead, they hope to sell when stocks become too expensive. But in our experience, it's nearly impossible for most investors to know when to sell.

Therefore, we want to focus on buying at the right time. Then we simply admit that we're not going to sell at the optimal point. We just can't predict how high stocks will go. And we want to capture as much of that upside as possible. Using trailing stops allows us to do this.

If you're not sure how to use them, please visit TradeStops.com for more information. Also, it's important to never give your stockbroker your stop-loss points. And never, ever base your stops on intraday prices. If you put your stops in the market (which is what happens when you give them to your broker)... events like a flash-crash can wipe you out.

If you remain dedicated to only buying stocks at a discount from their intrinsic value... if you become a connoisseur of value... and if you only make large investments when other investors are panicking, you should actually find that it's easy to keep a cash reserve.

But how many stocks should you own? What's reasonably diversified? I recommend never owning more stocks than you can completely understand and follow.

A good test is: Can you explain the stocks in your portfolio and why you bought them (the elevator pitch) to a friend without using notes or looking at your portfolio? If you can't, you don't know your investments well enough to own them or you're trying to follow too many.

You're not going to be able to find more than a handful of extraordinary investments at any given time. Why own anything that's not extraordinary?

Another good test for your portfolio is to make sure that there's not a single position that could cost you more than 5% of the value of your overall portfolio. Don't end up with so few large positions that a catastrophe in one stock wipes out all your other gains for the year.

The last part of our strategy (Step 5) to always beating the market is do everything you can to avoid the damage from fees and taxes, to maximize your long-term, compound returns.

Whenever possible, keep your assets in vehicles that allow you to compound your investments tax-free. Minimize trading and fees, which enrich your broker, not you. Look for companies whose management is well-known for doing tax-efficient deals and rewarding shareholders in tax-efficient ways. And always reinvest your dividends – either in the same companies or in new ones that offer better value.

Studies show that most investors perform terribly when managing their own assets. That doesn't mean that you can't do well. It does mean that the odds are stacked against you. So read and reread this list. Start living by it.

1. Never buy a stock whose intrinsic value you can't estimate reliably – and always get a big discount when you buy.

2. Become a connoisseur of value. Follow the cheapest, most hated segments of the market carefully. Wait and watch for moments of maximum pessimism, like Jay Carney's statement.

3. Allocate to value: Wait to make major investments when other investors are panicking and truly safe, outstanding opportunities abound.

4. Use good money-management techniques. Follow position-sizing guidelines and trailing stop losses. Never own more positions than you can carefully follow. Always keep a large cash reserve.

5. Do everything you can to avoid fees and taxes. Simply avoiding a 2% annual fee against your asset base (by not using money managers) is the No. 1 surest way to outperform your peers.

— Chapter 6 —

How to Invest in the World's Best Hedge Funds Without Paying Any Fees

Most people don't know that they don't have to settle for poorly run mutual funds or "buy everything" exchange-traded funds.

There are a handful of nearly secret investment funds that trade on the public market, have excellent track records, and treat their shareholders with great care and respect. Best of all, outside of paying a one-time brokerage fee, it costs nothing to own these funds.

I am going to detail the funds you can join and the secret "backdoor" way you can buy them. The summary is pretty simple: You can invest alongside the best and brightest investors in the world... You can gain substantial tax advantages (in some cases) by doing so... And executing these trades is no more difficult (or more expensive) than simply buying a stock.

So far in this guide, I've given you: seven ETFs that you can safely own. They will give you a diversified portfolio and beat the global stock market indexes handily.

Then I wrote about the three sectors I believe outside, passive investors (aka you) should focus on if you're going to do your own investing: insurance (profitable underwriters), capital-efficient businesses (especially those with addictive products), and resource stocks, when you can see that a commodity price cycle is making a major change in direction.

In these sectors, the most important, market-moving information is widely available, easy to understand... and largely ignored. In chapter 5, I wrote about how I "time" the market by focusing on intrinsic value, investor sentiment, and managing asset allocation.

Let's start there. Do you have any of your assets being managed by David Einhorn? What about Dan Loeb? Maybe you have cash with Prem Watsa or Carl Icahn. What about Sardar Biglari? He's one of the most talented young activist investors in the world. Do you think having at least some of your long-term savings with these guys would be a good idea?

I would argue that even if you're a professional investor and working on your portfolio full-time, it's unlikely that you're going to produce long-term results on par with these guys. They're the best in the world and they have the best analysts working for them, guys in their 20s and 30s who are blindingly smart and working 80 hours a week.

There are three reasons why more investors don't invest with these guys.

First, obviously, most people don't know how. They think they have to have millions to get into their hedge funds. They don't know that many of the most successful investors in the world offer their portfolios to public market investors.

The next problem is harder to solve: These holding companies typically have complex structures that make them very difficult to analyze and understand. I'll do what I can for you to show you how to make sense of them. But if you're going to invest in these firms, you really have to read their annual reports and their quarterly reports.

You should really go to the annual meetings, too. There's no substitute for looking these guys in the eye and hearing about their plans.

Finally... you have to be prepared for significant volatility. These guys are essentially leveraged financial firms. That means when a cold wind blows in the financial sector, these stocks are going to get "blown around."

Remember... Warren Buffett's Berkshire Hathaway saw its share price drop 50% twice during Buffett's tenure (1974 and 2000). The intrinsic value of Berkshire Hathaway didn't change much at all.

With these kinds of companies, you have to really understand what you own and what it's worth. The public-equity markets do a terrible job at pricing these kinds of companies.

Let's start with the most famous – Carl Icahn. There's a public vehicle that owns essentially all of Icahn's investment assets – Icahn Enterprises

(IEP). The company owns his direct investments, including eight casinos and other interests in railcars, steel, packaging, and real estate.

Roughly half of the company's assets are invested in Icahn's hedge funds, which include offshore funds that don't have to pay capital-gains taxes in the U.S. He personally owns 87% of the stock, which has a market capitalization of $12 billion and holds around $8 billion in net debt.

Over the last 10 years, Icahn has grown the book value of this business at an annualized rate of 18%. Currently, the stock trades at a significant 97% premium to book value...

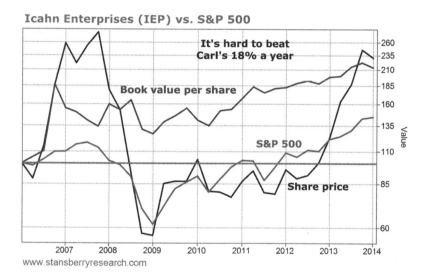

Icahn Enterprises (IEP) vs. S&P 500

www.stansberryresearch.com

The next most famous member of this group is probably David Einhorn. He's the founder of Greenlight Capital, a hedge fund that's value-oriented and also shorts stocks to hedge its exposure to the stock market – the same strategy I follow in my *Investment Advisory*.

Einhorn launched his hedge fund in 1996 with less than $1 million... and now manages around $10 billion. He launched a "captured" reinsurance company in 2004. Public-market investors can now buy shares of Greenlight Capital Re (GLRE), Einhorn's Cayman Islands-based reinsurance company. The insurance company underwrites profitably and invests 80% of its float back into Einhorn's hedge fund.

Since GLRE's inception in 1996, Einhorn has returned almost 20% a year to his investors. This reinsurance operation has seen its book value grow 19% a year. It currently trades at a 17% premium to book value...

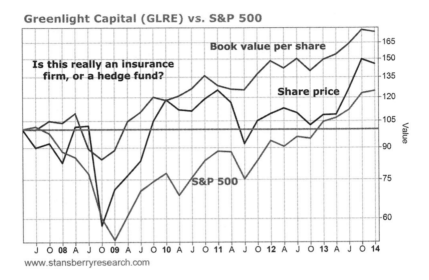

Greenlight Capital (GLRE) vs. S&P 500

Activist investor Daniel Loeb has a similar reinsurance firm set up in Bermuda. It's called Third Point Reinsurance (TPRE). Since inception in 1995, Loeb's Master Fund has returned more than 20% a year to its investors, making Loeb one of the greatest investors of this era.

His insurance company will underwrite profitably (although it hasn't yet) and invest its float in Loeb's funds, which are hedged with short positions, again, like my newsletter. There's a very short operating history here, as the reinsurance company only went public in New York last year. But so far, Loeb has grown its book value 35% annually. Currently, Third Point Re trades at a 13% premium to book value.

These first three investors are well-established and have proven their "chops" in a wide variety of markets and investments. The next investor I'd like to introduce you to hasn't done that... yet. I believe he's on his way to becoming a financial titan, and it may well pay huge dividends to hop on the boat before he's as big as an Einhorn or a Loeb.

His name is Sardar Biglari. His company is Biglari Holdings (BH).

Like Buffett, Biglari holds an annual meeting worth attending every year that features a tough Q&A session that lasts for hours. He, like Buffett, also writes annual letters that are brilliant. But unlike Buffett, he's known for being arrogant and doesn't suffer fools gladly... at all. Naturally, I like him.

Whatever you think of his personality, his track record is among the best in the world. He used a private investment fund to take over and turn around fast-food chain Steak & Shake, a move that required tremendous financial risk-taking and true operational excellence.

Biglari is one of the few executives who can operate at a high level both on the financial side and on the business side – something that Sears Holdings CEO Eddie Lampert, for example, has failed to do so far.

Biglari began to funnel Steak & Shake cash flows into activist campaigns (against fellow restaurant Cracker Barrel). And more recently, he bought his first insurance company (First Guard Insurance).

Out of all the young guys in finance these days, Biglari is the most fascinating... and I believe he will become the most successful.

The company is still small – the market cap is less than $1 billion. It holds little net debt. Over the last 10 years, Biglari has grown the firm's book value 12% annually. I believe, as his insurance operations ramp up, this figure will grow substantially, pushing annualized results up to 16%-18% annually. Currently, Biglari Holdings trades at a 21% premium to book value.

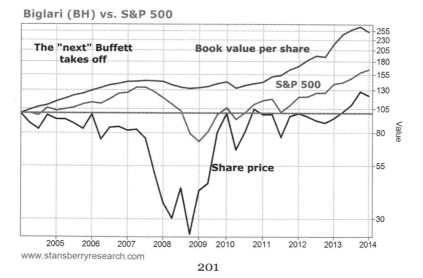

Biglari (BH) vs. S&P 500

The last "secret" fund I'd like to show you isn't a secret at all. It's a well-known insurance company – Fairfax Financial – headquartered in Toronto. What makes Fairfax unusual is that like Buffett's Berkshire Hathaway, the company invests most of its insurance float in value stocks. Its chief investment officer – Prem Watsa – is one of the world's leading value investors.

As an example of the contrarian ideas Watsa follows, he's now the largest holder of Blackberry stock – the totally out-of-favor cell-phone company. He also owns large positions in Sandridge Energy, one of the most overleveraged new oil and gas companies in the U.S. Sandridge was created by Aubrey McClendon's former Chesapeake Energy business partner, Tom Ward.

Like he did at Chesapeake, Ward borrowed too much money at Sandridge to buy too many marginal oil and gas properties. The result was a stock that fell from $60 to less than $5. Investors finally kicked him out and have slowly repaired the balance sheet and increased production to levels where the company is producing significant amounts of cash flow (more than $1 billion is expected in 2014).

This situation is classic Watsa. Over the last 10 years, Fairfax Financial has grown its book value 10% annually, using no net debt and carrying large amounts of cash. Currently, Fairfax Financial is trading at a 25% premium to book value.

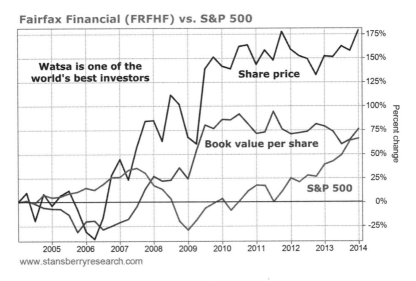

Fairfax Financial (FRFHF) vs. S&P 500

www.stansberryresearch.com

202

What should you do with this information? First, read whatever you can from these companies' public filings. Fairfax Financial, for example, has to report its positions in a 13F each quarter, giving you a free look at what one of the world's best value investors is buying.

Right now, there's one stock that makes up 40% of his U.S. equity portfolio. Sure, I could tell you the name of the stock, but there's no such thing as teaching. There's only learning. Just Google "Fairfax Financial, 13F." Figure it out yourself. You'll learn something.

And obviously, I recommend buying shares of these firms. They will grow their book value at a faster rate than you will grow your overall portfolio. Nothing is certain, of course... but the odds favor these investors in a massive way.

Here's a tip: From time to time, these shares trade for less than book value. That's because most investors don't understand insurance stocks or because, in Biglari's case, most investors simply think he's going to fail in his efforts to turn around or take over new businesses.

I don't think you should buy these stocks today. Financial stocks and financial operators have had huge runs higher. What you should do is wait, read, meet, and learn. By that, I mean watch the stocks carefully. Read their quarterly and annual reports. Attend their annual meetings. (Buy one share so you can attend.)

Learn what makes these businesses work... and when you feel comfortable that you really understand what they do and why, begin to invest. Do your best to buy when other investors won't. And try to pay less than book value.

You might also wait to see when these financial gurus – Einhorn, Loeb, Watsa, Biglari, etc. – begin to buy their shares. If you're patient, you'll get those opportunities.

Here's another tip. During periods of market uncertainty, these stocks will fall – usually more than the market falls. That means the prices on options for these stocks will tend to be rich. That makes these stocks great vehicles on which to sell put options. You can sometimes garner huge premiums, which can greatly reduce your acquisition cost. This strategy can reduce the cost of buying stocks like these by 25%-50% over the course of a year.

Chapter 7

How to Find the Best Conditions in the World for Investors

Do you think the current macroeconomic conditions in the United States are optimal for equity investors?

I don't. Optimal conditions for equity investors last existed in the U.S. in the late 1970s and early 1980s. At one point during that period, real interest rates reached as high as 10% a year in the U.S. and Treasury bonds were offering investors nominal yields as high as 15%.

With fixed income offering such large returns, equity valuations collapsed. At one point in the early 1980s, you could have bought oil major Exxon for less than five times earnings and gotten a dividend yield of nearly 8%.

We have almost the opposite conditions today. Real interest rates in the U.S., Europe, and Japan are currently negative. So much excess capital is in these bond markets that the sovereign borrowers no longer need to offer any effective rate of return. Central banks have flooded these markets with capital.

These conditions are terrible for equity investors, as valuations can become untethered from earnings. Stocks become expensive. And make no mistake...

U.S. stocks are expensive right now. So part of my advice has been to wait until the general conditions are more favorable to long-term investors. That's what I mean when I write about "allocating to value" and only making large commitments when other investors are panicking.

On the other hand... why wait? You can find developed equity markets all around the world in countries where property and contract laws are enforced and Western accounting is common. Isn't it possible that optimal conditions for equity investors exist somewhere?

Everyone has the ability today to invest in markets all over the world. Country-specific exchange-traded funds (ETFs) offer cheap and easy access to most developed markets in the world. And you can invest in some high-quality foreign companies that list their shares on the New York Stock Exchange.

Also, no law prohibits you from buying shares on foreign exchanges... And obviously, sometimes foreign markets are far more attractive than ours.

Since 2000, the number of Americans holding a valid passport has doubled. Today, more than 110 million Americans hold a passport – roughly 30% of the population.

Sadly, that doesn't mean most Americans have any real appreciation for foreign countries or cultures. It only means that post-9/11 Americans were forced to carry a passport to cross the borders with Canada and Mexico. I'm sure that far less than 30% of U.S. investors consider buying foreign stocks or investing in foreign stock market ETFs.

That doesn't make any sense to me. Some readers will think it's risky to invest outside of the U.S., where our laws and courts might not be able to protect investors. To me, that kind of thinking is laughable. It pretends that there's something particularly noble or efficacious about our legal system. If you believe that, you've never been involved with it.

Meanwhile, the facts are almost the opposite of what most Americans believe. It's far riskier to hold all your investments in one country and one currency. That's especially true when conditions are as poor as they are today for equity investors in America.

We recently launched two new foreign-oriented newsletters. *Global Contrarian* is a "blood-in-the-streets" look at the world's most completely "blown-out" equity markets.

Our *Global Contrarian* editor, Kim Iskyan, is the most experienced and well-traveled financial writer in the world today. He helped build stock exchanges across the former Soviet Union in the 1990s. Since then, he has covered emerging markets for hedge funds and investment banks. He has spent his adult life traveling the world, building relation- ships with bankers, brokers, and investors.

Who else could offer you insights into Iran's emerging stock market? Who else would travel to Ukraine in the midst of a war to find high-quality, dirt-cheap investments? Who else jumped on a plane to Thailand as soon as martial law was declared? Kim did. I'm extremely proud of his work in *Global Contrarian.*

There's nothing like it available, at any price, anywhere else. It is a must-read for any serious investor.

However, right now, I want to explain how our other international publication works. *Stansberry International* starts with the same approach as our *Stansberry's Investment Advisory.*

We look for high-quality, capital-efficient businesses and "Trophy Asset" stocks... but we're only looking for these kinds of investments in markets where conditions are optimal for equity investors. I don't believe this kind of investing is risky at all. I believe it's far safer than buying stocks in an overpriced U.S. market.

But look... I'm not trying to sell you a newsletter. I've promised to only give you the most valuable information I can in this book... the strategies and ideas that I would want you to give me if our roles were reversed.

Whether you subscribe to *Stansberry International* or not, I want you to understand why I hired Brett Aitken – a well-traveled, New Zealand-born business analyst living in Barcelona – to help me cover the most attractive global markets. And I want you to know the secret to our approach.

First: Like it or not, America is shrinking in terms of the global economy. When I was born (1972), the U.S. made up about 70% of the world's economy. By the time my sons have children, the U.S. economy will only represent about 20% of global gross domestic product (GDP).

Many countries around the world are growing faster than the U.S. Many countries around the world have much larger potential markets. These places will offer excellent investment opportunities, ones that will often be better and safer than buying U.S. stocks.

Giving up these opportunities automatically by never considering them is like trying to win a wrestling match with one arm. You might win. But even if you do, it would have been a hell of a lot easier with both arms.

Brett and I maintain a simple spreadsheet that covers all the investable markets in the world – places with well-established capital markets and companies that are listed on the New York Stock Exchange.

The core of our strategy relies on only two variables: real interest rates and equity valuations. We're looking for markets that reward capital (high real interest rates) and offer low equity prices. These are the markets that offer ideal conditions – just like the U.S. did in the early 1980s.

Let me show you what our database shows us right now and tell you what it means. In the chart below, we've circled the area that contains the most attractive markets. These are markets that offer both high real interest rates and low valuations.

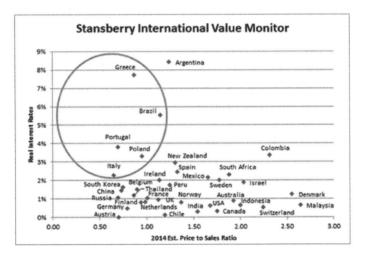

To better compare markets around the world with many different types of companies, we use the broadest measure of valuation – a price-to-sales ratio – to plot the chart. But we consider three measures of valuation in total – price to sales, price to book value, and price to earnings. There are, of course, problems with all these measures of valuation when looking at specific companies. But using them to compare "meta-data" across markets is fine.

Ideally, we'd like to see real interest rates above 10% and extremely low valuations – price to sales less than 0.5x, price to book around 1x, and price to earnings less than 10x. We saw those conditions a year ago in Greece.

In 2013, I suggested buying the Global X FTSE Greece 20 Fund (GREK), which holds a basket of Greek stocks, based on conversations I had with my friend, Erez Kalir. Erez, who runs the Ironbark Investments hedge fund, had visited the country and was extremely bullish on its prospects.

To hedge the trade, I also suggested "pairing" a long position on Greece by shorting the iShares MSCI France Fund (EWQ), which, naturally, holds a collection of French equities.

If you had made the trade, you would have ended up making more than 50% in a year on Greece, while you would have lost about 25% on the France short. Just keep in mind... we didn't intend to make money shorting France. We simply figured that Greece would do better than France. And it did.

The net gain was still great – better than 25% in a year. And that was from a fully hedged trade – you had no net exposure to stocks or Europe.

How Our Long-Greece/Short-France Trade Worked Out

When we see perfect conditions for equity investors, buying country-specific ETFs is fine. But in the long term, we can do even better by buying the best companies in these markets. So for us, Step 1 is to figure out where equity investors have their best opportunity.

For example, in Greece, we recommended buying Mytilineos Holdings. The company is basically the Berkshire Hathaway of Greece. It's a collection of lots of high-quality businesses. The head of Fairfax Holdings, Prem Watsa – the outstanding value investor I spoke about previously – has a large position in the company.

When we recommended the stock, it was trading at a 20% discount to book value, a price-to-sales ratio below 0.5x, and an incredibly cheap price-to-cash-flow ratio under 4x. This is as close to buying Exxon in 1981 as any security anywhere in the world right now.

In *Stansberry International*, we've recommended about a dozen different companies as of mid-2014, mostly in Greece and Spain. Going forward, Argentina seems most attractive.

I know you will probably never follow us into these markets. It's hard to grasp the idea that conditions that seem terrible for investors (high interest rates, collapsing stock prices) actually set the stage for a new bull market. The crisis Greece experienced from 2010 to 2012 created absurdly cheap stock prices. Today, the market is desperate for capital and offers investors outstanding returns.

Does buying into countries recovering from crises come with some risks? Yes, of course. But it also offers a high likelihood of outstanding profits. Investing in the U.S. – where stock prices are high, interest rates are low, and a debt crisis still looms – might "feel" safe. But it isn't safe at all.

It's far better to invest in markets where low prices and high interest rates more than compensate investors for risk, than to invest in markets where conditions are terrible for capital and there's zero compensation for risk.

By the way, this strategy isn't new. Lots of successful investors – like Sir John Templeton in the 1960s, Quantum Fund's George Soros and Jim Rogers in the 1970s and 1980s, and Tiger Fund's Julian Robertson in the 1990s – made a lot of money over the years following this global strategy.

I know it works. And I know it would work for you, if you were simply willing to try it. If you're too afraid to consider it right now, I understand. Here's what I suggest. Try just buying a tiny stake. Literally one share. See how it goes. See if it's really as scary as you think. If you'll just try it, I'm sure you'll come to agree with me: It's a lot easier to win a wrestling match with both arms.

Oh... one more thing. I've gotten to know Jim Rogers a little bit over the years. He was kind to me early in my career. And he has been a guest on my *Stansberry Radio* podcast a few times. One of the real secrets he shared to Soros' success in foreign markets shocked me...

Jim says that when they'd go into foreign markets after a crisis, they'd always buy the highest-quality companies – the "banks and brewers" – and they'd always buy a similar amount of the worst stocks, stuff that was almost out of business. Buying the best and the worst was their secret.

It worked because a few of those worst businesses would recover, resulting in astronomical profits, which would more than cover the losses on the ones that didn't make it. It's a cool idea... something I would have never thought to try without the tip from Jim. Obviously, the key is small position sizes and diversification across several risky opportunities.

Chapter 8

The Advanced Course:
The Only Way I Like to Trade Options

Fair warning. The secret I'm about to tell you is dangerous.

I'm going to show you how (and when) to make an absolute killing in the markets – profits that are unreasonable. I'm going to show you how I use options.

And if you use these ideas in the right way, you can produce hundreds-of-percent profits routinely and safely. But if you're careless, lazy, or greedy with these ideas... they will destroy your savings.

Let me start with some important parameters...

You should only use these techniques I'm going to show you on high-quality companies (companies with great brands, great assets, or both). And you should only use these ideas when you are 100% certain the value of the company far exceeds its current quoted price.

If you couldn't testify before Congress – with enough supporting evidence – that a fair price for the business is at least 50% more than the quoted price, don't even think about using these techniques.

Likewise, **never... ever... put more than 10% of your capital at risk in any of these trades**. You can make a lot of money with these ideas, but they will produce volatile results. You cannot handle this kind of volatility unless you're using the proper position sizes. **Don't have enough capital? Don't do the trade**.

(Please... read the last paragraph again before you continue – especially the last sentence: If you can't accurately value the business, if you aren't certain of what it's worth, or if you don't have enough capital to maintain the position at less than 10% of your portfolio, don't do the trade.)

My strategies involve using options. That statement ends the conversation for most of my readers. And that's really fine. You can be successful as an investor if you never, ever trade an option. On the other hand, if you want to make really large gains, you must use options. The key to success is never to pay for them. I think you'll agree that there's nothing wrong with taking a speculative position – like a call option – if you don't pay for it.

Let me show you exactly what I mean, using a real recommendation that we published in my *Stansberry Alpha* service. This isn't a sales presentation. I simply want to show you what I believe is the right way to use options – to use them in a way that greatly reduces your risk, greatly enhances your leverage, and can provide enormous returns on the capital you invest into the trade.

To start... you must find a security that features world-class assets and is deeply undervalued. Even as late as the end of 2012, that wasn't hard to do in the U.S. market.

For example, we'd been following the shares of MGM since mid-2008. The company, as you surely know, owns most of the major hotels on the Las Vegas strip. In the mid-2000s, it decided to build the most expensive, privately financed residential development in the history of the United States – the $9 billion City Center.

The project increased the number of MGM-owned hotel rooms in Las Vegas by about 50%. Some were even concerned that the Las Vegas airport didn't have the capacity to bring in enough people to fill these hotels and condos.

It was far too much new capacity at exactly the wrong time. We thought it was possible the company would go bankrupt. But we also knew if the company got additional capital, the stock would soar...

That's what happened in 2009: Wealthy oil-backed investors from the Middle East bought half of City Center. Then, during the years that followed, MGM restructured its debts, lowered interest costs, and made bankruptcy unlikely.

At that point, we needed to see one last sign before investing – a rebound in hotel rates, occupancy, and sustained revenue growth.

By 2012, MGM revenue hit a new all-time high and the company's assets were valued on the books at $27 billion. Meanwhile, the company had a market capitalization of only $10 billion. You could argue that the company was worth three times more than its stock price. Prior to the crisis, MGM had a market capitalization of $25 billion.

We recommended the stock in the July 2012 issue of my *Investment Advisory*. It was one of the best investment opportunities I had seen in my career. It was the kind of opportunity that can result in big gains in a short amount of time.

With the company's balance sheet back on solid footing, I didn't believe there was any material risk in owning the stock. So... how could we turn this good of an opportunity into a killing?

In the December 2012 *Stansberry Alpha* (our second issue), we recommended selling a put option on the stock with a strike price of $10 that expired in January 2014. A put option is nothing more than a promise to buy 100 shares of stock at a fixed price ($10, in this case) for a certain period of time (until January 2014).

The main advantage of selling a put – of merely promising to buy the stock instead of actually buying it – is leverage. To allow you to sell this option, brokers ask for a deposit that assures you can meet your potential obligation. (The amount of leverage you can get depends on your broker, but the legal minimum is only 20%.)

With a strike price of $10, investors only had to put up $2 per share. And this is hard to believe, but it's true... other investors were willing to pay us $1.36 in exchange for this promise to buy the stock.

In our view, **selling a put is less risky than buying a stock**. It requires less capital (in deposit). And assuming you pick a strike price that's below the market, your effective "buy-in price" will be lower than the price of the stock at the time of your trade.

In this case, instead of buying MGM shares at $11, we were promising to buy at an effective price of $8.64. We calculate our effective "long" price by simply subtracting the fee we got in exchange for selling the put from the strike price ($10 − $1.36 = $8.64). I hope you can understand that buying a stock at $8.64 a share is less risky than buying the same stock at $11 a share. Thus, selling **puts allows us to take less risk, but in a leveraged way**.

The main problem with merely selling puts is that it's too safe. Yes, we're earning $1.36, while only putting up $2. That's an instant return of 68%. But we're only earning that return on a sliver of our capital. If the stock takes off like we expect, we're giving up a lot of potential upside. We don't have enough capital in the trade, and we don't have an unlimited upside position.

To capture more of that upside, we can spend a portion of the cash we received for selling a put (called the "premium") to purchase a call option. A call option is the opposite of a put option. It gives us the right (but not the obligation) to sell 100 shares of stock at a fixed price for a fixed period of time.

In this case, we recommended buying a $15 call on MGM that also expired in January 2014 for just $0.57. This gives us the option of opening a 100-share position in the stock at $15 a share. Of course, we'd only exercise that if the stock traded for more than $15 by January 2014.

As you can see, it costs almost nothing. And it requires zero deposit. Considering that even after buying this call option, we're still getting $0.79 in net premium for our promise to buy MGM (39.5% return on invested capital), I'd consider that a nearly free option.

I get that it's not actually free. But the point is, I don't believe you should ever buy an option unless you've found a way to finance it. And when I can earn an immediate return of nearly 40% on the capital I've tied up in this trade and get a call option... the call is close enough to free for me.

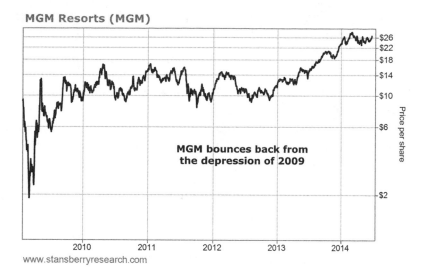

MGM Resorts (MGM)

MGM bounces back from
the depression of 2009

www.stansberryresearch.com

After our recommendation... MGM's stock did well. After about six months, it was up more than 50%. In June 2013, we decided to take some of our profits off the table, mostly because we grew concerned about the U.S. corporate bond market (which was crashing). In hindsight, we sold much too soon. But even so, let's look at what happened.

First, we never had to put any additional capital into this trade. The stock never traded for less than our $10 strike price. Thus, we never got a "margin call."

To close the position, we had to buy back the put we'd sold. The price of the put had fallen to $0.22, leaving us with a net premium of $0.57 per share (after you account for the cost of the call option we bought). That's a reasonable 28.5% gain in about six months.

The big gains came from the call option... We sold the call option for $1.81 per share. Keep in mind, we got this call option essentially for free. We generated all the cost ($0.57) when we sold the put. So in total, on a $2 cash investment, we earned a net premium of $0.57 and call option profit of $1.81. That's a total return of $2.38 – a 119% return our $2 cash investment in only six months.

In real dollar terms, let me show you how this might have worked in a real portfolio. Let's assume you have a $100,000 portfolio. Putting $2,000 into this trade (on margin) would have allowed you to sell 10 put contracts on MGM at our recommended $10 strike. (Remember, each contract covers 100 shares.) That's only 2% of your entire portfolio.

But this trade is using 20% margin, which means your total potential margin requirement is $10,000. That's 10% of your portfolio. You're within our recommended risk boundaries. If your portfolio is smaller, you simply sell fewer put contracts. (With a $50,000 portfolio, for example, you would sell five contracts as a maximum position size.)

To sell the 10 contracts, you'd give your broker $2,000 in cash. He'd immediately hand back to you $1,360 in put premium, from which he'd take another $570 to purchase the $15 calls. You'd start out the trade up $790, almost $800 in the black. That offers you a considerable "margin of safety" – an instant return of 40% on the capital you've invested in the trade.

Realize, like in a real estate deal, if you are forced to meet a margin call, your return will decrease. That's why it's critical that you limit your trading only to deals where you can have a tremendous amount of certainty in the underlying value.

To close out this trade, you would have bought back the put option you sold earlier – but they only cost $0.22 per share to buy back. On 10 contracts, that totals $220. Thus, you earned a net option premium of $570 on your $2,000 investment in only six months.

That's nearly 30%. That's a great return. But it's not the real "juice."

The big gains came from the call option, which you were able to sell for $1.81 per share. On 10 contracts, that's $1,810. To find your total return, you simply add the money you made on net premium ($570) with the money you made from the call option ($1,810).

If your calculator works like mine, that's a total return of $2,380 in about six months on an investment of $2,000, or nearly 120%.

— Chapter 9 —

Why You Should Never Buy Stocks

Over the last eight chapters, I've worked hard to give you a summary of what I believe are the most valuable ideas, strategies, and secrets I've learned (so far) during my career in financial research.

I've saved the most valuable secret for last: **I firmly believe that most individual investors should never buy stocks**.

That probably seems ironic coming from a guy who has spent his entire adult life researching investments and advising people from around the world on markets. I've recommended hundreds of different stocks. Was I lying then, or am I lying now?

No, I'm not lying. In fact, I'm telling you such a huge secret, it could easily lead you to never buy a stock again. I'm telling you this secret for the simple reason that it's what I would like you to do if our roles were reversed.

That's how I do business. And I know that if I serve my readers in this way – by that exacting standard – everything else in my business will take care of itself. The folks who appreciate my efforts will stay. The folks who don't weren't going to renew their newsletter subscriptions anyway.

So whatever you decide to do with this information, I hope you'll read carefully and think deeply about what I'm about to tell you.

Stocks can be fantastic investments. I try my best to only recommend the ones that will make you a lot of money. But the hardest part of my job is overcoming unbelievably bad management teams. If more investors really knew what happened in the offices of the CEOs of publicly traded companies, I promise... you'd never buy a stock again.

I've personally seen deal after deal executed – involving billions of dollars – that had zero chance of ever creating any shareholder value. Likewise, I've seen CEOs refuse to make simple, logical, and necessary changes or divestitures that would have, in some cases, saved their companies from bankruptcy.

I'm involved in a situation right now where I'm begging the management team of a great business to make a decision about its asset portfolio that's completely obvious, even to an outsider like me.

And yet, the suggestions – which are clearly in the best interest of all shareholders – will likely be treated like an attack, an affront on the dignity of the management. The truth, of course, is that if the management team had any real dignity, it would be doing a much better job of managing its asset base.

The fact is, 90% of the time, CEOs do what's in their best interest – damn the torpedoes. That means trying to garner as many assets as possible, in the blind hope that something good eventually happens with one of them. And often enough, what's in their self-interest is diametrically opposed to what their shareholders deserve.

What won't you often see? Management teams giving themselves an honest appraisal. Not even Berkshire Hathaway founder Warren Buffett. He wrote publicly for many years that the test of his skill as a manager was to outperform the S&P 500 on an after-tax basis for any rolling five-year period.

For the first time in his entire career, he didn't achieve this goal. So what did he write in his 2014 letter? Going forward, he promised to beat the S&P 500 every six years.

He didn't say anything about his disastrous investment into ConocoPhillips at the top of the oil market in 2008 or his $10 billion investment – the largest of his entire career – into lackluster tech giant IBM. Instead, he made excuses about the size of his portfolio and "moved the goalposts" – something he had spent his career criticizing other CEOs for doing.

Keep in mind, Buffett could spin off any of the assets he doesn't want to manage anymore and quickly regain a growth rate that's more appropriate. But will he ever do so? Not a chance. And that's from the management team at one of America's most respected and beloved companies.

What can you do about it? Buffett recommends only buying businesses that, as he says, "could be run by monkeys." After all, he warns investors, "sooner or later, that's what will happen." Too bad nobody realized he was making a prediction about Berkshire.

Is that a cheap shot? I don't know. Probably. But it's amazing how every management team – even Buffett – can devise wondrous excuses for miserable performance. What can you do about it? Well, that's easy: Don't give them any cheap capital. They don't deserve it.

"All right, tough guy," you're probably saying. *"If we're not going to put our money into stocks, what should we do? We can't trade commodities... We'll get killed. We can't hold cash... The Fed is printing the dollar into oblivion. Fixed income? You must be kidding – how can anyone survive on earning less than 6% a year?"*

Yes, **the answer is fixed income**. And you won't be surprised to learn that it's a kind of fixed income that your broker probably won't sell you... at least, not easily.

It's a kind of fixed income that offers you incredibly high rates of income – more than 10% – and huge capital gains, too... capital gains that can rival (or even exceed) the largest gains you've ever made in stocks.

But before I get into the details of how to make this work for you, I want to pause for a moment and talk about why this works.

American managers act like capital is free. They make terrible capital-allocation decisions. Far from "allocating to value," they constantly allocate to popularity. As a result, they chronically overpay for super-low-quality assets. The way you can make this work for you is simple: You lend them the money.

Capital isn't free, of course. And if you take a more senior position in the capital structure (bonds versus stocks), you can make sure that you nearly always get paid. The management team doesn't have the option of whether to reward you for your investment or not. It must pay the coupon on your bond or else the company will go bankrupt, its assets will be sold, and its employees will be out of a job.

I would bet that more than 90% of my subscribers have never purchased an individual corporate bond. That's madness. If I could, I wouldn't let any of my customers buy stocks until they had invested in corporate bonds.

Bonds are far safer than stocks. The average recovery rate on corporate bonds in default is around $0.45 on the dollar, according to financial services firm Standard and Poor's.

No, you don't want to try to buy a bond of a company headed for bankruptcy. Of course not. Recovery in bankruptcy is always uncertain and there are no guarantees, especially not these days, when the government and the courts are doing crazy things.

But it's an indication that, for most bonds, at the very worst, you're going to get back a good portion of your money. That's especially true if you follow my advice, which is to never pay more than $0.70 on the dollar for corporate bonds. But... I'm getting ahead of myself.

There are really three things you have to know about buying corporate bonds the right way. The right way means:

1. You're going to get more than 10% a year in yield.

2. You can't lose more than 35% of your investment, no matter what.

3. There's an overwhelming likelihood that you'll make at least 100% total return over three years.

That's three times more than you'll make in stocks on average. The reality is, most individual investors make almost nothing (less than 3% annually) in stocks because they always sell at the worst possible time.

I say that based on studies like those done on mutual funds (by research firm Dalbar) and by a big study conducted on actual brokerage account results (by investment manager Blackrock).

Judging by our feedback e-mail and conversations I've had over many years with both investors and brokers, the same facts apply to most (not all) of my subscribers. My advice? At the very least, **make bonds the center of your portfolio going forward**.

When you own bonds instead of stocks, there are three layers that protect you from making bad decisions. **First, you don't have to worry about bonds going to zero (90% of the time).** You are legally entitled to your coupon payments and to your share of the company's assets if it can't pay you in full.

Second, if you learn to buy at the right time (when the bond market is in distress), you will receive large amounts of income. This makes it hard to lose money overall. Like the "rich man" in the famous Richard Russell essay, having a rich stream of income makes you patient and allows for you to wait until the perfect deal comes along.

And third, bond investments normally take several years to mature. This encourages you to avoid overtrading and, again, to wait until exceptional deals appear.

But rather than blather on more about theory... I'd like to show you a real example. We'll use MGM again, because it's a company almost everyone understands. The Las Vegas Strip-dominating hotel and casino company is one of our favorite "trophy asset" businesses.

If you take a look at the company's five-year share-price history, you'll discover that MGM's shares got clobbered during the 2008-2009 financial meltdown. The shares have since rebounded about 300% from their average price during 2009 (around $10).

I discussed why this happened in Chapter 8: The company built out a massive expansion (City Center) at exactly the wrong time. But it still had great assets it could easily sell and it didn't have too much debt.

In the middle of the crisis in 2009, the company sold one of its lowest-quality hotels (Treasure Island) for $14,000 per hotel room. Assuming it only got the same value for its more upscale hotels, the company's Vegas assets alone were worth far more than all its debts. And that assumes fire-sale pricing and ignores the company's substantial assets outside Vegas and in China.

MGM was suffering a liquidity crisis, not a solvency crisis. And that meant buying its debt was safe. You couldn't say the same thing about its stock. Investors had no idea if management would get new funding if it would be able to keep the "wolf" at bay.

Before buying its shares, you needed to wait until you could see sustained improvements in its revenues and cash flows. That's what we did.

On the other hand, buying its debt was always safe. Because no matter what stupid thing management did next, the hotels and casinos were still going to be there... And they were extremely valuable, as the 2009 sale of Treasure Island proved.

MGM Resorts International (MGM)

MGM shares have soared since the crisis (5-year chart)

www.stansberryresearch.com

By early 2009, MGM bonds were trading for less than $0.50 on the dollar. They hit bottom at $0.30 on the dollar. Of course, nobody can know when markets will bottom and what the best available price will be.

And we won't pretend that looking back we could have gotten the "low tick" in MGM's bonds.

But any price below $0.50 on the dollar would have qualified as a world-class opportunity. At that price, the yield on the bonds would have been 15% annually. That's like Santa Claus showing up at your office with a big sack of free money. Or as I like to say about really obvious investments: horse, meet water.

Only three years later, these bonds were trading back at "par" – 100 cents on the dollar. **Over three years, these fully collateralized bonds would have doubled your money.** And you also would have collected another 45% in coupon payments.

Earning 145% in three years – without taking any substantial financial risk – is a far better deal than buying any stock...

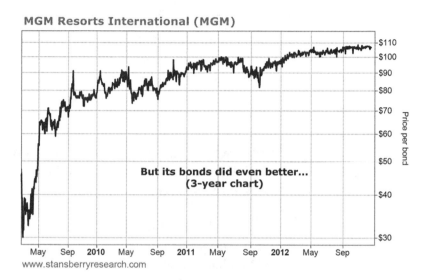

MGM Resorts International (MGM)

www.stansberryresearch.com

Sure, MGM's stockholders have done well, too. The stock is up about 150% over five years. But who knew back then if management could right the ship? Who knew what stupid thing it would do next? Who knew how long it would take?

That's the beauty of these deals... As bondholders, we truly didn't care what management did or didn't do. It was up to them to pay us or lose everything. It's like the movie *Goodfellas*. When the mob lends you money, you have to pay them.

Recall the scene in *Goodfellas* where the mobsters burned down the poor guy's restaurant? Oh, business is bad? Too bad, pay us. Oh, a bunch of jerks ran up big tabs and won't pay them? Too bad, pay us. Oh, someone burned down your restaurant? Too bad, pay us.

Bondholders have the same exact view. Oh, global financial crisis hurt your business? Too bad, pay us.

If those big returns available in stocks are too irresistible, there's nothing stopping you from combining equity and debt into a single position. If you're fairly confident that management can bail out the ship, you can simply buy shares with the discounted portion of the bond.

Corporate bonds typically trade in face values of $1,000. So if you bought MGM's bonds at $0.50 on the dollar, you would have had $500 or so to buy shares. At the time, the stock was trading for less than $10. To make the math easy, let's say you got shares at $10. So you have a bond with a $1,000 face value (purchased at $500) and 50 shares of stock for a total investment of $1,000.

Here's the best part: **No matter what happens to the shares, you're going to get all of your capital back because those bonds mature in 2016 and then the company has to pay you back your $1,000**.

Even though the stock was really risky back then, you were protected. By today, the bond would have paid you $375 in coupons... and it's trading at a premium to face value. And the shares would be worth roughly $26 each, or $1,300, for a total return of 167% over five years – far more than 30% a year. And again, you really didn't take any risk in this trade.

There are, of course, plenty of pitfalls and problems associated with investing in corporate bonds. The biggest problem is that high-quality assets like MGM's aren't often available as collateral on bonds yielding more than 10%, let alone 15%. There is, however, a regular cycle in the corporate-bond market...

Once every seven to 10 years, the market completely blows up. When bond liquidations start, even the highest-quality issuers will see their bonds trading at big discounts to par. A few rules of thumb can help you easily time these cycles.

First and foremost, you want to watch the spread between high-yield corporate bonds and U.S. Treasurys. This will generally tell you whether corporate bonds are distressed or trading in the clouds.

As you can see in the next chart, the spread between high-yield bonds and U.S. Treasury bonds has rarely been this small. The last time it was this small was 2007.

When capital is this cheap and easy, you simply must stand aside from this market, as far too many loans are going to be made to far too many low-quality companies. The result will be a huge wave of debt defaults at some point between 2015 and 2019. We can't know when it will happen – but we know it will happen. Just look back at history...

The "Spread"

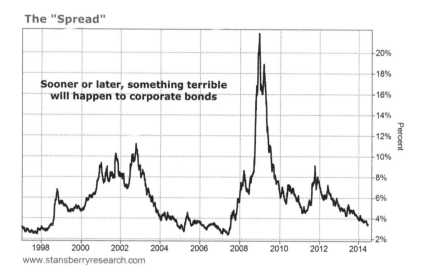

www.stansberryresearch.com

This chart, from the U.S. Federal Reserve, shows the spread (the difference) between so-called "risk-free" bonds (based on U.S. Treasury bonds with a similar duration) and the Merrill Lynch high-yield corporate-bond index. This is the standard measure of corporate credit conditions.

When the spread is low, credit is widely available and cheap. When the spread is high, credit is tight and can be incredibly expensive. Investors should wait to buy corporate bonds when credit is tight and attractive yields abound.

There's something about watching and waiting on the bond market to "roll over" that I really enjoy. This is a "when" investment, not an "if" investment. All we have to do is be patient. We know that the feckless, reckless, and stupid management teams running most American companies will borrow too much money and end up in a jam.

It happens every eight years or so. That's about perfect timing for patient investors, as most corporate debt is issued for periods of less than 10 years. You can "lock in" a solid rate of return buying bonds when they go on sale, are trading for less than $0.70 on the dollar, and pay more than 10% annually.

If you begin to do this, I promise, you'll buy far fewer stocks. **You'll make a lot more money as an investor. You'll take dramatically less risks. And you'll produce way more income**.

Now, I know a lot of you may be scratching your head at what I've written here. After all, no one has issued more adamant warnings about the bubble that has developed in the bond market. And yes... now is not the time to make big investments in the corporate-bond market.

But this essay isn't about what to buy today or tomorrow. I want you to recognize the incredible opportunity corporate bonds represent when the conditions are right, when you can get them at the right time and price. Remember, at some point, all markets turn around.

After the bond market collapses, most investors want nothing to do with fixed-income investments. That's when we find lots of great opportunities in this market... ones that meet all three of my guidelines for buying corporate bonds.

How do you buy bonds? And which exact ones should you buy? Don't worry. During the last cycle, we made 81%, on average, in 2009-2010. The Rite-Aid bond we recommended way back then is No. 2 in the Stansberry Research Hall of Fame at the bottom of every *Stansberry Digest*.

If you want to go forth on your own... remember to focus on companies with a lot of high-quality and easily marketable assets.

Judging collateral is a lot different than judging an operating business. You have to think like a pawn dealer: How hard would it be to unload these assets if the idiots running this business really screw the pooch? That's a far different question than figuring out a reasonable price to pay for future cash flows, or brand value, etc.

More and more, I believe bonds are far better investment instruments than stocks for most investors. The funny thing is, most brokerage firms make it difficult for individuals to buy high-yield corporate bonds.

Most won't even tell you what bonds are available. And most will only sell you the bonds you want if you're able to tell them the precise CUSIP number of the bond (its trading symbol).

That's the best indicator of all. Wall Street's smart money doesn't want you figuring out the best deals in the bond market, which, by the way, is vastly larger than the stock market. Interesting, isn't it?

How to Earn Crisis-Proof, Inflation-Proof Income Streams in the Stock Market

Chapter 1

The No. 1 Way to Invest for Retirement

By Brian Hunt, Editor in Chief, Stansberry Research

Porter note: There's a lot of interest in "crisis proof" investing these days.

It's no wonder this is a big topic. The 2008 financial crisis created extreme volatility and crashing prices. It took millions by surprise.

Now, people are asking important questions...

What investments can I own that will withstand a financial crisis?

What investments will help me collect safe income streams that will withstand inflation?

At Stansberry Research, we've thought a lot about these questions.

One of our top recommendations for "crisis-proofing" your portfolio is to own gold.

But there's an asset that has proven over many years to be an even better vehicle than gold for preserving and growing your wealth. We believe knowing about this asset is so important, we wrote a guide about it.

Part Ten of *America 2020* is this guide.

Written by my great friend and Stansberry Research Editor in Chief Brian Hunt, this guide will show you exactly how to put this asset to work for you... and how to start earning crisis-proof, inflation-proof income streams.

What I (Brian Hunt) am about to tell you is without a doubt the No. 1 way to invest for retirement.

Of all the investment ideas we've covered over the years, this stands head and shoulders above the rest. It's the strategy we urge our parents to use. It's the strategy we teach our children.

This strategy produces huge returns. It can turn thousands of dollars into millions of dollars. It's also very low risk. It will allow your investment portfolio to withstand any crisis (just like it did during the financial crisis of 2008).

Rather than worry about money and security in your retirement years, you can use this strategy to live an income-rich retirement.

The neat thing about this strategy is that anyone can use it. It's very simple. Many regular people have used this strategy to make huge fortunes in stocks. You can use it, too.

If you know nothing about the stock market except what is explained in this guide, you'll be a vastly better investor than almost everyone on Wall Street... or any MBA... or anyone on CNBC.

What I'm going to share with you is a "secret" in the sense that few people use it. It's really an "open secret." Nobody has it under lock and key. It's hiding under an invisible blanket of common sense.

When you start putting this secret to work for you, you'll "graduate" into a higher class of investors.

Before you read further, I'd like you to picture a tree...

Once you plant a tree, you don't have to do anything more with it. The tree sinks its roots into the ground and starts growing. All the tree needs is rain, air, and the nutrients in the soil.

You don't have to check on it every day. You leave it alone. You let the awesome forces of nature make the tree stronger and stronger as the years go by. The tree will provide fruit, beauty, and shade for you, your children, and your children's children.

Have that picture in your mind?

That's what using this investment strategy is like.

It's harnessing an unstoppable force of nature to safely build wealth, year after year.

With that picture in mind, let's get started...

Chapter 2

What's Truly Important for Growing Wealth in the Stock Market

If you're reading this, you've probably invested some money in the stock market. You probably have a 401(k), an IRA, or an individual brokerage account.

Once you invest some money, you'll probably start watching a little financial television. You'll probably read financial websites or a few investment magazines.

While reading and listening to financial media, you're sure to encounter dozens of "gurus" who promote lots of different market strategies... and make lots of big predictions. You're sure to see lots of news stories about the economy and the government.

It's a lot to take in. It can all be very confusing.

And for 999 out of 1,000 people, it is a distraction from what really leads to long-term success in stocks.

You see, the news you read in the paper or hear on CNBC is completely meaningless compared with the idea I'll share with you in this guide.

Most people watch the financial news and think they're doing something important. They're actually just wasting time and getting distracted from what's truly important for making big, safe returns in the stock market.

And what's truly important for growing wealth in stocks is the accumulation of elite, dividend-paying businesses purchased at reasonable prices.

That's it.

It's the most important idea.

It's the "king" of all investment ideas.

It's a thousand times more important than knowing what the economy is doing... or what the government is doing... or what's happening in the news.

Again... **what's truly important for growing wealth in stocks is the accumulation of elite, dividend-paying businesses purchased at reasonable prices**.

What is an elite business? How can you find it?

And how can one safely and surely generate wealth for you?

You'll find the answers in the pages that follow...

Chapter 3

The Traits of Elite Businesses

There's no set definition of an "elite business." But most smart people agree that elite businesses share some unique traits.

An elite business has a durable competitive advantage over its competitors.

For example, major discount retailer Wal-Mart has a durable competitive advantage because its huge global distribution network allows it to sell goods at unbeatably low prices. It's very, very difficult for smaller firms to compete against it.

An elite business usually has an outstanding brand name.

Coca-Cola is a good example. People associate Coke's logo and name with quality soda all over the world.

An elite business is often the largest business in its industry. When you run your business better than the competition, you usually can't help but become the biggest. McDonald's became America's biggest fast-food chain because it ran a better business than its competitors.

An elite business often sells "basic" products, like food, oil, soda, cigarettes, beer, mouthwash, razor blades, and deodorant. These are things that don't go out of style.

And here's something you don't often hear: **Most of the truly elite businesses sell habit-forming, or even addictive, products**.

If you look at the list of the 20 best-performing U.S. stocks from 1957 through 2003, you'll note many of them sold habit-forming products. It jumps right out at you.

For example, Phillip Morris is at the top of the list. It was the top-performing S&P 500 stock from 1957 to 2003. It sold cigarettes, which contain addictive nicotine.

Fortune Brands, which was called American Brands for a while, is on the list. It sold cigarettes and alcohol.

Coca-Cola and PepsiCo are on the list. They sold soda... which is a sugar- and caffeine-delivery vehicle.

Hershey Foods and Tootsie Roll are on the list. They sold chocolate and sugar. Wrigley is on the list. It sold sugary gum, like Big Red and Juicy Fruit.

People love a little sugar rush. It's habit-forming... even addictive.

Many drug companies are on the list. These names include Abbott Labs, Bristol-Myers Squibb, Merck, Wyeth, Schering-Plough, and Pfizer.

People get accustomed to taking certain drugs. Much of the time, those drugs are useful. Sometimes, they are not. I'm not saying they are good or bad. I'm simply pointing out that people get accustomed, even addicted, to taking them.

You can make the case that certain fast foods are addictive as well. Fast- food companies load their food with fat, sugar, and chemicals that make people want more. This is part of the reason McDonald's has been such a corporate success.

The businesses I just mentioned produced more than 13% annual gains for more than three decades.

Those returns are extraordinarily rare in the stock market. You won't find anything better.

An investment of $25,000 in a tax-deferred account that grows 13% per year for 30 years grows to nearly $1 million ($977,897).

Most companies can't sustain 13% annual returns for more than five years. **The businesses I just mentioned sustained those returns for de- cades**.

And the reason why they did so well is simple...

When people form a habit around a product, it goes a long way toward ensuring repeat business. People get used to certain brands, and they grow resistant to switching.

Also, when people get used to a product and the brand surrounding it, they are more likely to continue buying the product, even if the price increases a little. Both of these help companies sustain long-term sales growth and healthy profit margins. That's good for shareholders.

It's also important to know that when these companies hit upon the right recipes or the right mix of whatever it takes to make good products, they don't have to make large, ongoing investments in the business. They don't have to spend tons of money on more research and development.

Once Coca-Cola hit upon the recipe for Coke, it didn't have to change it. The same goes for Budweiser and Hershey and Tootsie Roll.

When you make a product that people love and develop habits around, you don't tinker with it. You don't have to spend a lot of money on new research and development. You don't have to buy expensive, high-tech equipment.

You can instead spend that money on things that will provide a high return on investment, like marketing, distribution, or manufacturing.

This means a larger percentage of revenues can be sent to shareholders.

Owning the world's top sellers of basic (often habit-forming) products is also ideal for investing in high-growth emerging markets like China and India.

Combined, China and India have about 10 times the population of the United States. Many of those people are at the level of economic development of

America during the 1940s... and they are getting a little richer every year. It's one of the biggest investment opportunities in history.

To invest in this trend, I don't want to try to guess what websites will get the most clicks... or what retailer will become popular. That's a very difficult game to play. Those business landscapes will change rapidly.

On the other hand, I'm confident those folks in China and India who are getting a little richer every year will want to enjoy the same habit-forming products Americans have enjoyed for decades.

They'll want to consume more branded soda, cigarettes, beer, liquor, and processed foods.

Owning elite global businesses that serve those growing markets makes a lot of sense.

(By the way... these global sellers of branded, habit-forming consumer goods are the kinds of businesses Warren Buffett, the greatest investor in history, always looks to buy. He's a longtime owner of Coca-Cola and candy maker See's Candies.)

— Chapter 4 —
The Secret of High Stock Market Returns

When a great business develops a durable advantage over its competitors, it often begins paying steady and rising dividends.

Dividends are cash payments distributed to a company's shareholders. They are often quoted in dollars per share, as in "Coca-Cola pays a dividend of $1 per share."

Dividends are also quoted in terms of a percent of the current stock price. This percentage is referred to as the "yield." You might say, "Coca-Cola pays a dividend yield of 3%."

In 2012, respected investment research firm Ned Davis Research produced a study that shows why investors should care **a lot** about dividends.

This study contained some of the most valuable data you'll ever see.

Understanding this data can make you rich. Not understanding it can cost you years of wasted effort and lots of money.

You shouldn't invest one dime in the stock market unless you understand it.

In the study, Ned Davis Research analyzed the returns of various types of stocks within the benchmark S&P 500 Index from 1972 to 2010.

In this study, Ned Davis Research placed each S&P 500 stock into one of four general categories.

Category one: Companies that were paying dividends and increasing them.

Category two: Companies that were paying dividends, but not increasing them.

Category three: Companies that were reducing or eliminating dividend payments.

Category four: Companies that didn't pay a dividend.

In other words, Ned Davis Research categorized stocks based on their policies of paying cash to shareholders.

You could say two of the categories (reducing dividends or not paying dividends) consisted of businesses that were generally **not good at paying cash to shareholders**.

You could say one category consisted of companies that were **OK at paying cash to shareholders** (paying dividends, but not increasing them).

You could say the fourth category consisted of stocks that were **great at paying ever-increasing amounts of cash to shareholders** (paying dividends and raising them).

According to the study, companies that paid growing dividends returned an average of 9.6% per year. Companies that were paying dividends but not increasing them returned an average of 7.4% per year.

Companies that did not pay dividends returned an average of 1.7% per year. Companies that were cutting or eliminating their dividends returned -0.5% per year.

Here is that data shown in a table:

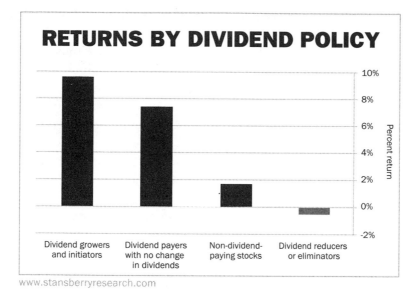

RETURNS BY DIVIDEND POLICY

Dividend growers and initiators | Dividend payers with no change in dividends | Non-dividend-paying stocks | Dividend reducers or eliminators

Percent return: 10% 8% 6% 4% 2% 0% -2%

The results of the nearly 40-year study are clear: Companies that are great at paying cash to shareholders perform better than companies that stink at it. As the ability to pay dividends increases, returns go up. As the ability to pay dividends declines, returns go down.

Continuously rising dividends is a mark of business excellence. **And business excellence translates to big shareholder returns**.

"Wait a minute," you might say. "If I only buy stocks that pay dividends, won't I miss out on big growth-stock winners that invest their profits into growing the business instead of paying it to shareholders?"

Yes, you will.

By sticking with dividend-paying stocks, you will miss out on investing in the next Starbucks... or the next Facebook.

But remember, for every winner like Starbucks, there are 1,000 failed coffee chains.

For every winner like Facebook, there are 1,000 failed websites.

It's very, very unlikely that the average investor will be able to consistently find these companies early on… and hold them for years. Even trained professionals struggle (and often fail) to pick those kinds of winners.

It's *much, much more likely* the average investor will be able to consistently identify companies that sell boring, basic products like soap, burgers, and beer… and pay ever-increasing dividends.

By now, you know those companies are usually found in your refrigerator, cupboard, or medicine cabinet.

If you're interested in building long-term wealth in the stock market, consider changing the way you look at different stocks.

Consider placing each business you come across into one of four simple categories.

And only buy businesses that fit into one of those categories: The rising dividend category.

Does the business pay rising dividends, stagnant dividends, no dividends, or is it reducing dividends?

If the business doesn't pay continuously rising dividends, pass on it.

Buy the best and ignore the rest!

Chapter 5

The Shortcut for Finding the World's Best Businesses

Now... you can spend a lot of time searching for "elite businesses."

You can study for days and learn how to analyze stocks. You can spend hours going over financial statements.

But if you're like a lot of people, you don't have the interest or the time. You've got a job and a family, and they keep you busy.

The good news is, there's a shortcut around doing all that work.

You can simply look for businesses that have increased their dividends for at least 10 years in a row.

Remember, dividends are cash payments distributed to a company's shareholders. Only businesses with durable competitive advantages can pay increasing dividends for more than a decade.

Out of the more than 5,000 publicly traded businesses, less than 5% meet this high standard of quality.

These businesses are the beachfront real estate of the stock market.

Some legendarily profitable and stable members of the "dividend raiser" club include Coca-Cola, McDonald's, and Wal-Mart... as well as health care company Johnson & Johnson, payroll services company Automatic Data Processing, technology maker IBM, global courier FedEx, soft-drink maker PepsiCo, manufacturing conglomerate 3M, consumer-products maker Procter & Gamble, and gas giants Chevron and ExxonMobil.

The longer the string of consecutive dividend increases, the more impressive it is. Only truly fantastic businesses with durable competitive advantages can increase their dividends for 20, 30, or even 40 consecutive years.

As of 2014, Wal-Mart has increased its dividend payment every year for 41 years. ExxonMobil has increased its dividend payment every year for more than 30 years. Coca-Cola has increased its dividend payment every year for more than 50 years.

These businesses paid and increased their dividends through recessions, government shutdowns, wars, and real estate busts. They paid their dividends during the dot-com bust. They paid their dividends during the 2008-2009 financial crisis – the ultimate dividend "stress test."

In terms of consistency, these firms rank just behind the rising sun.

Companies with more than 10 or 20 years of consecutive dividend increases are the strongest, safest companies in the world. As I mentioned, many of these firms sell "basic" products like medicine, soda, food, candy, cigarettes, toothpaste, and deodorant.

Ordinary companies can't raise their dividends for 10 or 20 consecutive years. In fact, they probably won't even exist that long. This is because their business models are shaky, unpredictable, and vulnerable to competition.

The average investor will spend lots of time chasing hot tips from brokers, coworkers, and relatives. He'll chase "get rich quick" schemes. He'll try to pick stocks based on chart patterns. He'll stay up at night worrying about the risky stocks he owns.

It's bizarre behavior when you realize there is a group of elite, dividend-paying businesses available to him. He's choosing Spam over filet mignon.

Instead of owning risky stocks, I like the predictability of owning robust, reliable businesses like McDonald's and Coca-Cola.

I can't pick the next hit website, the next miracle drug, or the next retail fad. But I know it's very, very likely that folks will keep eating burgers, drinking soda, and brushing their teeth.

Again, you can spend lots of time learning how to analyze businesses... You can spend a lot of time searching for them.

Or you can simply "weed out" more than 99% of stocks by focusing on companies with long strings of consecutive dividend increases.

Several lists of these companies are compiled each year. One is called "Dividend Achievers." It's the list of companies that have increased their dividends for at least 10 consecutive years. As of 2014, there were 239 members of this list.

Another list is called "Dividend Aristocrats." It's the list of companies that have increased their dividends for 25 consecutive years. As of 2014, there are only 54 members of this list.

You can think of these lists as "cheat sheets" for finding the world's best businesses.

You work hard for your money. Don't abuse it by investing in low-quality businesses.

Instead of buying unproven businesses based on whims, chart patterns, and hot tips, demand quality from the businesses you buy.

One of the greatest indicators of business quality is at least 10 years of consecutive dividend increases. This is the blue ribbon worn by the best public businesses.

— Chapter 6 —

A Strategy for Buying Elite Businesses at Bargain Prices

Although the businesses I've described are the best on Earth, they suffer share-price selloffs from time to time.

Sometimes, these selloffs are caused by short-term, solvable problems within the individual companies.

Sometimes, these selloffs are caused because the overall stock market goes down in value.

These selloffs are almost always opportunities to buy these firms at bargain prices and start collecting steady dividend payments.

When you buy a car, you want to pay a good price.

When you buy a house, you want to pay a good price. You don't want to overpay. You don't want to embarrass yourself by getting ripped off. You want to get value for your dollar.

Yet... when people invest, the idea of paying a good price is often cast aside.

They get excited about a story they read in a magazine... or how much their brother-in-law is making in a stock, and they just buy it.

They don't pay any attention to the prices they're paying... or the value they're getting for their investment dollars.

Warren Buffett often repeats a valuable quote from investment legend Ben Graham: "*Price is what you pay, value is what you get.*"

That's a great way to put it.

Like many investment concepts, it's helpful to think of it in terms of real estate...

Let's say there's a great house in your neighborhood. It's an attractive house with solid, modern construction and new appliances. It could bring in $30,000 per year in rent. This is the "gross" rental income... or the income you have before subtracting expenses.

If you could buy this house for just $120,000, it would be a good deal.

You could get back your purchase price in gross rental income in just four years ($120,000 / $30,000 = 4).

In this example, we'd say you're paying "four times gross rental income."

Now... let's say you pay $600,000 for that house.

You would get back your purchase price in gross rental income in 20 years ($600,000 / $30,000 = 20).

In this example, we'd say you're paying "20 times gross rental income."

Paying $600,000 is obviously not as good a deal as paying just $120,000.

Remember, in this example, we're talking about buying the same house.

We're talking about the same amount of rental income.

In one case, you're paying a good price. You're getting a good deal. You'll recoup your investment in gross rental income in just four years.

In the other case, you're paying a lot more. You're not getting a good deal. It will take you 20 years just to recoup your investment.

And it's all a factor of the price you pay.

It works the same way when investing in a business...

You want to buy at a good price that allows you to get a good return on your investment. You want to avoid buying at a bloated, expensive price.

This is a vital point.

No matter how great a business is, **it can turn out to be a terrible investment if you pay the wrong price**.

If you're not clear on this point, please read through the home example again.

When it comes to buying elite businesses that raise their dividends every year, you can use the company's dividend yield to help you answer the important question: "*Is this business trading for a good price or a bad price?*"

Here's how it works...

When a stock's price goes down and the annual dividend remains the same, the dividend yield rises.

For example, let's say a stock is $50 per share and pays a $2-per-share annual dividend. This represents a yield of 4% (2 / 50 = 4%).

If the stock declines to $40 per share and the dividend payment remains $2 per share, the stock will yield 5% (2 / 40 = 5%).

When a selloff causes an elite dividend-payer to trade near the high end of its historical dividend-yield range, it's a bargain... and it's a good idea to buy shares.

Remember, these companies pay the world's most reliable dividends.

Their annual payouts only go one way – UP.

When an elite dividend-payer's share price suffers a decline of more than 15%, consider it "on sale" and buy it.

For example, in the late 2008/early 2009 stock market decline, shares of elite dividend-payer Procter & Gamble fell from $65 to $45 (a decline of 30%).

Procter & Gamble is one of the world's top consumer-products businesses. Every year, it sells billions and billions of dollars' worth of basic, everyday products like Gillette razors, Pampers diapers, Charmin toilet paper, Crest toothpaste, Bounty paper towels, and Tide laundry detergent. It has raised its dividend every year for more than 50 years.

Investors who stepped in to buy this high-quality business after the market decline could have purchased shares at $50.

In the five years that followed, Procter & Gamble climbed to $80 per share. Its annual dividend grew to $2.57 per share.

This annual dividend represented a 5.1% yield on a purchase price of $50 per share... and that yield will continue rising for many years.

Owning one of the world's best businesses... earning a 5.1% yield on your shares... and collecting a safe income stream that rises every year...

Buying the best at bargain prices is a beautiful thing.

If you have the interest, time, and know-how, you can track these businesses yourself. You can find all the information you need on many free financial websites. Or you can simply pay an advisor or research firm to do it for you.

Remember, you can make a bad investment in a great business if you pay a stupid price. View your investment purchases just like you would the purchase of a home, a car, or a computer.

Get good value for your investment dollar. And when an elite dividend-payer sells off for some reason, see it as an opportunity to buy quality at a bargain price.

Chapter 7

Why Owners of Elite, Dividend-Paying Businesses Don't Worry About 'the Market'

When you realize that your No. 1 job as an investor is to accumulate as many shares as possible of elite, dividend-paying businesses, you "graduate" into a higher class of investor.

You also experience a lot less stress than the average investor.

Let me explain...

Few people belong to this exclusive class because most folks are obsessed with short-term gratification.

They pore over tiny market movements, news releases, CNBC clips, and other things that are meaningless in the "big picture."

These people are always busy trying to get the market to do something for them... instead of using the greatest power in all of investing.

That power is TIME.

And if used properly, time causes extraordinary things to happen to your portfolio.

Time allows you to earn huge yields from elite, dividend-paying businesses.

Time makes it so you don't care about the moods of the stock market.

Here's how it works...

Let's say you buy Reliable Breweries (a fictional company), which is an elite, dividend-paying business, for $20 per share. It has increased its dividend payment every year for the past 30 years. It pays a 5% annual dividend, or $1 per share.

Now, let's say that dividend grows at 10% per year for the next 10 years. (This rate of dividend growth is common with elite businesses.)

After 10 years of growing at 10% per year, your annual dividend is now almost 13% of your initial investment. After 15 years of growing at 10%, your annual dividend is 21% of your initial investment. After 20 years of growing at 10%, your annual dividend is 34% of your initial investment.

Now... do you think a guy earning a safe 13% yield with one of the world's best businesses cares about a stock market correction?

Do you think he cares about a 5% decline in home prices? Do you think he cares about some economic news story on financial television?

No way.

He's comfortable knowing that no matter what the stock market does, folks are still going to be buying products from Reliable Breweries.

He knows the broad market could decline by 20% and he would still get that 13% yield on his shares. They could shut the market down for a year and he'd still get his money.

That's the peace of mind accumulators of elite, dividend-paying businesses enjoy.

By combining the power of an elite, dividend-paying business and the power of time, you are able to generate massive yields on your original investment. You just have to let time work its magic.

This concept is very important to understand... so please think about a few more questions...

If you're earning a 13% (and growing) yield on a stock, do you care if the share price falls 10%?

Do you care if oil climbs $10 or $20 per barrel?

Do you care that this guy or that guy is predicting a stock market decline?

No way.

No matter what stories the media is hyping, the "biggies" of the corporate world — companies like McDonald's and Coca-Cola — will still be No. 1 in their industries.

They'll still have giant, insurmountable competitive advantages.

They'll still have thick profit margins.

They'll still generate huge cash flows.

They'll still direct a portion of those cash flows to shareholders through ever-increasing dividends.

Their longtime shareholders will still earn 13%-plus yields on their original investments.

For most folks, trying to trade in and out of stocks takes up too much time. It generates high fees. It produces losses. It causes sleepless nights. It drains mental energy.

But if you own a collection of elite, dividend-paying businesses, you won't worry about much.

You sleep well knowing that all you need is TIME.

Time allows dividend growth to work its magic.

Think of it like planting a money tree... and remember what I said at the start of this letter:

> Once you plant a tree, you don't have to do anything more with it. The tree sinks its roots into the ground and starts to grow. All the tree needs are rain, air, and the nutrients in the soil.

> You don't have to check on it every day. You leave it alone. You let the awesome forces of nature make the tree stronger and stronger as the years go by. The tree will provide fruit, beauty, and shade for you, your children, and your children's children.

Buy an elite, dividend-paying business at a good price, leave it alone, and it will grow large in your portfolio.

Given enough time, it will throw off 5%... 10%... even 25% annual dividends on your original purchase price.

It will grow into a large money tree you and your family can enjoy for decades.

As you go through your investment career, keep in mind your No. 1 job: **To accumulate as many shares as possible in great businesses purchased at reasonable prices**.

Chapter 8

Elite Businesses Allow You to Harness the Power of Compounding

Getting paid a reliable and growing dividend is a great thing.

As I mentioned, over time, it can produce 13%-plus yields on your initial investment.

But there's a way to make this great idea even better...

Elite, dividend-paying companies like McDonald's and Coca-Cola allow you to harness the most powerful investment force on the planet.

This force is called "compounding."

Compounding occurs when you place a chunk of money into an investment that pays you a return on your money. But instead of taking the returns and spending them, you "reinvest" them... and buy more of the investment.

By doing this, your dividends earn more dividends and your interest earns more interest.

You can think of compounding returns through dividend reinvestment like rolling a snowball down a hill. As the snowball gets larger, it's able to gather more snow... which enables it to get larger... which enables it to gather more snow... which enables it to get larger... and so on.

Eventually, you build a snowball the size of a house.

Compounding is the ultimate way for the "little guy" to safely build wealth in the stock market.

Given enough time, a good compounding vehicle (like a Dividend Aristocrat) will turn tens of thousands of dollars into millions of dollars.

For example, let's say you invest $10,000 in an investment that pays a 5% dividend. Your intention is to compound over the long term.

In Year 1, a $10,000 investment paying 5% in dividends will pay you $500. You take this money and buy $500 more of the investment.

In Year 2, your investment has grown to $10,500 but still earns 5%. That year, you'll earn $525 in dividends... which you can use to buy more of the investment.

In Year 3, your investment has grown to $11,025, but still earns 5%. At the end of that year, you'll earn $551.25 in dividends... which you can use to buy more of the investment.

You can see how it works.

After 20 years of compounding, a stake of $10,000 throwing off 5% in dividends will grow to $26,533.

After 30 years, it will grow to $43,219.

After 40 years, it will grow to $70,400.

And remember, this number assumes no further money is added to the program as the years go by... or that the investment produces any capital gains.

As you can see, long-term compounding produces extraordinary effects.

It's a very important concept for young people to learn... because they have the power of TIME on their side.

The longer you can compound, the more extraordinary the results.

The following example shows just how extraordinary the results can be...

Consider two investors, Robert and Sally.

Robert opens a tax-deferred retirement account at age 26. He invests $3,000 per year in this account for 40 consecutive years. Robert stops contributing at age 65. His account grows at 9% per year.

Sally opens a tax-deferred retirement account at age 18. She invests $3,000 per year in this account for eight consecutive years. After those eight years, she makes no more contributions to her retirement account. Her account grows at 9% per year.

The results of these two approaches are below... and they are extraordinary:

Age	Robert		Sally	
	Contribution	Year-End Value	Contribution	Year-End Value
16	$0	$0	$0	$0
17	$0	$0	$0	$0
18	$0	$0	$3,000	$3,270
19	$0	$0	$3,000	$6,834
20	$0	$0	$3,000	$10,719
21	$0	$0	$3,000	$14,954
22	$0	$0	$3,000	$19,570
23	$0	$0	$3,000	$24,601
24	$0	$0	$3,000	$30,085
25	$0	$0	$3,000	$36,063
26	$3,000	$3,270	$0	$39,309
27	$3,000	$6,834	$0	$42,847
28	$3,000	$10,719	$0	$46,703
29	$3,000	$14,954	$0	$50,906
30	$3,000	$19,570	$0	$55,488
31	$3,000	$24,601	$0	$60,481
32	$3,000	$30,085	$0	$65,925
33	$3,000	$36,063	$0	$71,858
34	$3,000	$42,579	$0	$78,325
35	$3,000	$49,681	$0	$85,374
36	$3,000	$57,422	$0	$93,058
37	$3,000	$65,860	$0	$101,433
38	$3,000	$75,058	$0	$110,562
39	$3,000	$85,083	$0	$120,513

40	$3,000	$96,010	$0	$131,359
41	$3,000	$107,921	$0	$143,182
42	$3,000	$120,904	$0	$156,068
43	$3,000	$135,055	$0	$170,114
44	$3,000	$150,480	$0	$185,424
45	$3,000	$167,294	$0	$202,112
46	$3,000	$185,620	$0	$220,303
47	$3,000	$205,596	$0	$240,130
48	$3,000	$227,369	$0	$261,742
49	$3,000	$251,103	$0	$285,298
50	$3,000	$276,972	$0	$310,975
51	$3,000	$305,169	$0	$338,963
52	$3,000	$335,905	$0	$369,470
53	$3,000	$369,406	$0	$402,722
54	$3,000	$405,923	$0	$438,967
55	$3,000	$445,726	$0	$478,474
56	$3,000	$489,111	$0	$521,536
57	$3,000	$536,401	$0	$568,475
58	$3,000	$587,947	$0	$619,637
59	$3,000	$644,132	$0	$675,405
60	$3,000	$705,374	$0	$736,191
61	$3,000	$772,128	$0	$802,448
62	$3,000	$844,889	$0	$874,669
63	$3,000	$924,199	$0	$953,389
64	$3,000	$1,010,647	$0	$1,039,194
65	$3,000	$1,104,876	$0	$1,132,721
Less Total Invested		**-$120,000**		**-$24,000**
Net Earnings		**$984,876**		**$1,108,721**
Return on Money		**8-fold**		**46-fold**

Sally made just eight contributions of $3,000, for a total of $24,000 invested. Robert made 40 contributions of $3,000, for a total of $120,000 invested.

However, Sally started at 18 years of age and Robert started at 26 years of age. Sally started eight years earlier. And those eight extra years of compounding are worth more than all of Robert's 32 years of extra contributions.

Despite a much smaller total contribution, Sally ended up with more money... and a much, much bigger return on her investment.

This example shows why compounding is such a powerful idea to teach children. They have the ultimate advantage of TIME.

This piece of knowledge is one of the greatest financial gifts you could ever give your children.

In order to put your compounding plans on "autopilot," consider using something called a **"dividend reinvestment plan," also called a DRIP**.

A dividend reinvestment plan is just what it sounds like. It's a plan that takes the dividends you earn and reinvests them into buying more stock.

Once you set up a DRIP, you don't have to do a thing. Again, think of a DRIP as a way to put your compounding plan on "autopilot."

You can ask any stock broker to institute a DRIP for you. Any reputable online broker will do it for you. It's a simple process. You can find directions on your broker's website or call the customer service department.

Chapter 9

Elite Dividend-Payers: The Cure for the Biggest Mistake Income Investors Make

Amateur investors often bring up a common objection to buying elite, dividend-paying businesses.

Acting on this objection often leads them into very risky investments.

Most elite, dividend-payers sport annual dividend yields in the neighborhood of 2%-5%. And remember, these yields are incredibly safe and reliable. They rise every year.

In addition to elite dividend-payers, the stock market contains groups of businesses that pay annual yields of 6%... 8%... 10%... even 12%.

The amateur looks at these numbers and says, "Why buy a business that yields 4% when I can buy one that yields 8%?" And then the amateur makes one of the biggest investment mistakes in the world.

He "chases" yield.

There's a classic piece of investment wisdom about "chasing yield." It goes: *"More money has been lost chasing yield than at the barrel of a gun."*

"Chasing yield" is the act of buying specific stocks simply because they offer high yields... while ignoring vital business factors.

Some businesses engage in risky business ventures or take on lots of debt in order to pay high yields. Finance and real estate companies often do this.

Some businesses own oil and gas wells and pay dividends from the production. Those dividend payouts are often totally dependent on oil and gas prices staying elevated.

They can be incredibly volatile.

These businesses are usually very dangerous for the average investor.

For example, there is a group of companies whose chief business activity is borrowing money at low interest rates... and then using that borrowed money to buy mortgages that pay higher interest rates. They make money from the "spread."

One of the largest and most popular of these companies is Annaly Capital Management.

Annaly is probably operated by good people. But because it borrows lots of money to buy mortgages, its business – and its dividend yield – is very volatile. Small changes in the business (like how much it has to pay to borrow money) can cause enormous changes in shareholder returns.

Here is a chart of Annaly's dividend payments from late 2007 to late 2014. As you can see, these payments are incredibly volatile.

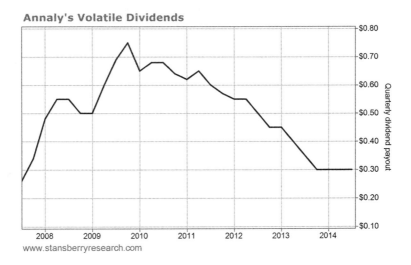

The volatile nature of Annaly's dividend payments leads to volatile share-price movement. Next is a chart of Annaly's share price during the same time period (late 2007 to late 2014). Note the drop from more than $20 per share to $10 per share.

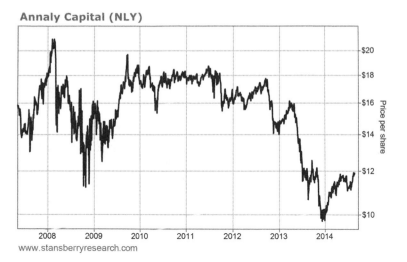

Annaly Capital (NLY)

Or... consider the performance of the San Juan Basin Royalty Trust from 2011 to 2013. At the time, this trust was one of the biggest and most popular trusts that owned natural gas assets.

From mid-2011 to mid-2012, the price of natural gas dropped around 50%. Because the San Juan Basin Royalty Trust derived its revenue from natural gas, its shares dropped as well. As you can see from the next chart, they fell from nearly $28 to around $12 per share.

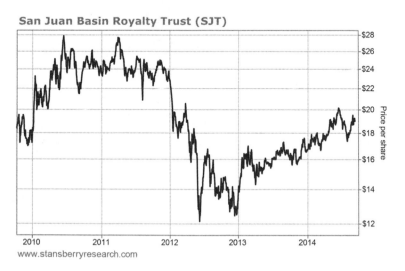

San Juan Basin Royalty Trust (SJT)

Also consider the performance of Enerplus. In 2011, it was one of the biggest and most popular owners of oil and gas wells... and paid dividends out of production.

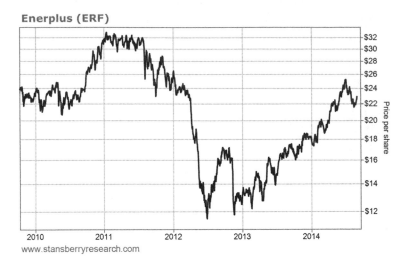

Enerplus (ERF)

www.stansberryresearch.com

In 2011, crude oil fell from $110 per barrel to $85 per barrel. This decline helped crush Enerplus shares. As you can see, they fell from $32 per share to less than $12 per share.

The examples of Annaly, San Juan Basin, and Enerplus are not unique. And I'm not picking on these particular businesses.

This story plays out over and over in the stock market... with dozens and dozens of companies.

Unsuspecting investors see a company offering a very high yield and they buy it. They don't do any research to determine if the business model is risky or not. In almost every case, it is.

Some investors are good at timing their purchases of these volatile business-es. They buy them when they are deeply out of favor with most investors.

However, the average investor almost always buys these businesses at the wrong time: near peaks in share prices. He picks up 8% in dividends and then loses 30% on the share-price drop.

The individual investor is much, much better off owning stable businesses that pay out reliable and growing dividends. You don't trade in and out of elite dividend-payers. There's no frequent buying and selling. There's no worry that the share price will fall 30%. There's no dangerous leverage.

You simply buy them and begin building wealth the low-stress way.

While the dividends and share price of Annaly were bouncing up and down, elite dividend-payers like Coca-Cola and McDonald's were paying steady and rising dividends.

Chapter 10

Why Elite, Dividend-Paying Businesses Are the Ultimate 'Wealth Defense'

If you're like a lot of folks, you're worried about inflation... and the danger it presents for people saving for retirement or already in retirement.

You might also be worried another financial crisis is wrecking your investments.

If you're one of these people (and there's a good chance you are), the "no brainer" decision for you is to own the elite, dividend-paying businesses I describe in this guide.

Owning an elite, dividend-paying business is a good inflation defense because the business' strong brand and loyal customer base will allow it to raise prices along with inflation. Its dividend will often increase at a faster rate than inflation, so the value of your income stream remains intact.

These companies are safer, better places to park long-term wealth than any currency or any government bond. They are better for parking long-term wealth than gold.

There are several major reasons why they're incredible vehicles for your money...

For one, **buying a great business is extremely cheap and easy**. You don't get hit with big fees and commissions when you buy and sell them. You can't say that about real estate or art. Buying a great business through an online broker will cost you less than lunch at most restaurants.

Two, **holding a great business is extremely cheap and easy**. It's as easy as holding cash in the bank. There are no storage costs. There are no transportation costs. You don't have to get a safe-deposit box or a home safe, like you might do with gold or diamonds.

Three, **shares of a great business are liquid and freely traded**. There's a huge market for these business. It's open most every business day.

Four, elite, dividend-paying businesses also **pay out reliable, extremely safe income to their shareholders**. (You already learned this, but I just thought I'd remind you.)

And finally, great businesses are great inflation-defense vehicles. They have long histories of rising in value when paper currencies decline in value.

This is one of the most important aspects of these stocks...

You see, governments have a long history of debasing currencies.

When governments want to pay for big social programs or wars, they often print up extra currency units (like dollars). Every currency unit that is printed devalues the existing currency units. This is called "inflating" the money supply.

Inflation is a way for governments to quietly clip small bits of value from your bank account and your wallet.

Inflation is one of the greatest dangers a person saving for retirement faces. It can crush the future buying power of the money you save today.

This is why owning great businesses is so important. Great businesses hold their value through inflationary periods.

The world's most successful investor, Warren Buffett, figured this out a long time ago.

Buffett urges people who are worried about paper-currency declines to own world-class businesses. He figured out a long time ago that owning great businesses is a better inflation-defense than owning gold.

I agree with Buffett on this point. The numbers prove it. Owning great businesses is better than gold when it comes to preserving and growing wealth over the long term.

Consider that from the start of 1990 through early 2014 – a time period that includes booms and busts for both stocks and gold – gold returned 222%.

Now consider during that time...

- ExxonMobil returned 1,573%.
- Wal-Mart returned 1,775%.
- Coca-Cola returned 1,270%.
- Johnson & Johnson returned 2,213%.
- McDonald's returned 1,660%.

(Note: These numbers factor in dividend reinvestment.)

Keep in mind... these companies were well-established enterprises in 1990. It wasn't like you were buying speculative startups.

The numbers are clear. **Owning elite businesses that generate consistent dividends is a better long-term strategy than owning gold**.

If you're concerned about inflation or another financial crisis, I encourage you to think about this idea... and how the world's greatest investor, Warren Buffett, approaches it.

Sure... own some gold. Own some real estate. But keep in mind the proven wealth-building power of owning the world's best businesses.

Chapter 11

A Beautiful View of Your Investment Backyard

As great as the idea of "planting money trees" is, you're unlikely to use this strategy at the start of your investment career.

The reason is that this investment approach is boring. You're simply buying the world's best businesses and holding them for years and years.

Checking in on these businesses usually amounts to hearing about modest increases in profit... and increases in dividend payments.

These companies typically don't report big "breakthroughs" that could double profits in a year. They just report steady sales growth and relentless dividend increases. They do this year after year after year.

This approach doesn't provide much "action." And when it comes to investing, most people seek action. They pursue lots of hot tips. They look to strike it rich with one big win. They simply can't bring themselves to pursue such a boring strategy.

You also might get overwhelmed by all the information out there on how to invest. There are dozens of investment gurus touting their strategies. There are hundreds of investment books. There are thousands of investment websites.

If you achieve great results with other strategies, congratulations. But if you're one of the many investors who has found lots of "action" – but little success – with exciting strategies, I hope you'll come around to the idea in this guide.

Once you come around and commit to a lifetime of accumulating elite, dividend-paying businesses purchased at reasonable prices, you'll eventually have a beautiful view of your "investment backyard"...

At the end of your investment career, you'll have a large collection of elite, dividend-paying businesses... throwing off regular cash dividends.

You'll have an orchard of money trees in your backyard.

The branches of your money trees will be heavy with fruit every year. One "tree" will yield 20% on your original investment... one will yield 25% on your original investment... one will yield 30% on your original investment... and so on.

Broad market corrections won't concern you. The latest government drama won't concern you.

You'll sleep well at night knowing your elite businesses will continue to pay out regular cash dividends.

You'll have a large and growing portfolio of the world's best soda companies, the world's best energy companies, the world's best food companies, etc.

Instead of a fancy art collection or a car collection, you'll have a money tree collection.

For emphasis, let's go over it one last time...

If you commit to a lifetime of accumulating elite, dividend-paying businesses purchased at reasonable prices, you're virtually guaranteed to build significant wealth in the stock market. And you will build that wealth safely.

This is the world's No. 1 way to invest for retirement.

It's the closest thing there is to having money trees growing in your backyard.

Think of These Steps as Insurance for a Storm

Please take the simple steps necessary to protect yourself and your family.

I hope you'll take the research my team and I have spent an incredible amount of time and money preparing seriously. I know in my heart it will be one of the best financial moves you ever make. And I want you to remember one more important point:

All of the steps I am recommending are simple, cheap, and easy… at least for now.

But as you know from your own experience, "storm insurance" and provisions get much more expensive, and even impossible to buy, as a storm approaches.

Think about what happens every time there's a hurricane or snowstorm. As the storm nears, it becomes impossible to buy batteries, water, or a generator, anywhere within 150 miles of where the storm is likely to hit.

Well, it's the same with safeguarding your money. There has been a huge crisis going on in America for years, and it is about to get much worse.

Few people are thinking about these financial moves, so they are still simple and easy to execute. But as the coming financial storm nears, and more people clamor to save themselves, these moves will become extremely expensive, and even impossible, to make.

You want to take action now.

Because the thing to remember about a currency collapse is that it happens gradually… gradually… gradually… and then very suddenly.

Americans and foreign investors are clearly losing faith in the U.S. dollar. Over the past few years, it has been a progressive and steady decline. But when the final collapse occurs, there will be no announcement. There will be no warning. It will be devastating and swift.

So please do the smart and prudent thing: Take the necessary actions now to protect yourself and your family.

How to Follow Porter Stansberry's Latest Research and Ideas

In 1999, Stansberry Research founder Porter Stansberry launched the company's flagship newsletter, *Stansberry's Investment Advisory*. Hundreds of thousands of investors in 120 countries read Porter's work each month.

In his newsletter, Porter has predicted the most promising emerging trends and the most influential economic forces affecting the market – with uncanny accuracy.

From the Internet boom and bust... to the real estate boom... to the collapse of natural gas prices... to the oil boom in the U.S., these and other accurate predictions have led *Stansberry's Investment Advisory* subscribers to incredible gains.

But that was just the beginning. What Porter is most well-known for is how he helped his *Investment Advisory* readers avoid the big disasters associated with the 2008 financial meltdown.

Starting in late 2007, Porter repeatedly warned of the financial crisis about to come. In August 2008, he told readers: *"GM is now in a death spiral."*

By December 2008, GM was down 88%, trading at an all-time low. And in June 2008, Porter predicted Fannie Mae and Freddie Mac, the two largest and most-leveraged owners of U.S. mortgages, would go bankrupt in the next 12 months.

Just three months later, both enterprises had to be bailed out by the government.

Porter's work on Fannie Mae and Freddie Mac was considered so accurate, financial reporter Alan Abelson wrote about his analysis in the popular "Up and Down Wall Street" column in *Barron's* – calling it "remarkably prescient... Nothing, as far as we can see, has happened to contradict his dire prophesy."

Subscriber Robert R. wrote us to say, "I knew that our country was headed in a very wrong direction, I did not know how to minimize the personal impact to our family... But you have given me many ways to help protect my family financially."

"You're my new American hero," Harry J. told us.

"Your investment ideas and commentary should be mandatory reading for anyone in Washington involved with the current debacle, as well as the morons on Wall Street whose overleveraged house of cards has now collapsed. Thanks for all you do for us," wrote subscriber Ben T.

Stansberry's Investment Advisory costs just $49.50 per month. And Porter offers an unconditional, 100%-money-back guarantee to new members. To try it out for four months without risking a penny, **call 888-261-2693**.

Or you can go directly to our *Stansberry's Investment Advisory* order form by typing this unique, safe, and secure website address into your Internet browser: **www.sbry.co/b4ggps**.

More from Stansberry Research

The World's Greatest Investment Ideas

The Stansberry Research Trader's Manual

The Doctor's Protocol Field Manual

High Income Retirement:
How to Safely Earn 12% to 20%
Income Streams on Your Savings

World Dominating Dividend Growers:
Income Streams That Never Go Down

Secrets of the Natural Resource Market:
How to Set Yourself up for Huge Returns
in Mining, Energy, and Agriculture

The Stansberry Research Guide to Investment Basics

The Stansberry Research Starter's Guide for New Investors

The Living Cure:
The Promise of Cancer Immunotherapy

Dr. David Eifrig's Big Book of Retirement Secrets